Mid-Century Modern

Mid-Century Modern
Living with mid-century modern design

Judith Miller

Miller's Mid-Century Modern
by Judith Miller

First published in Great Britain in 2012 by Miller's,
a division of Mitchell Beazley,
imprints of Octopus Publishing Group Ltd,
Endeavour House, 189 Shaftesbury Avenue, London WC2H 8JY
www.octopusbooks.co.uk
www.octopusbooksusa.com

Editorial Consultants: Marc Allum (Furniture), Mark Hill (Glass)

Miller's is a registered trademark of Octopus Publishing Group Ltd
www.millersonline.com

An Hachette UK Company
www.hatchette.co.uk
Distributed in the US by Hachette Book Group USA,
237 Park Avenue, New York NY 10017 USA
Distributed in Canada by Canadian Manda Group,
165 Dufferin Street, Toronto, Ontario, Canada M6K 3H6

ISBN 978 1 84533 693 6

A CIP record of this book is available from the British Library
and the Library of Congress.

Printed and bound in China

Publisher: Alison Starling
Designer and Jacket Designer: Pene Parker
Art Director: Jonathan Christie
Head of Editorial: Tracey Smith
Production Manager: Peter Hunt
Project Editor: Joanne Wilson
Chief contributors: Marc Allum, Katy Armstrong, Mark Hill, John Wainwright
Copy editor: Alexandra Stetter
Proof Reader: Kate Fox
Indexer: Hilary Bird

Value codes

Throughout this book the value codes used at the end of each caption correspond to the approximate value of the item. These are broad price ranges and should be seen only as a guide to the value of the piece, as prices for costume jewelry vary depending on the condition of the item, geographical location, and market trends.
The codes are interpreted as follows:

A	under £50	under $75
B	£50–100	$75–150
C	£100–200	$150–300
D	£200–300	$300–450
E	£300–400	$450–600
F	£400–500	$600–750
G	£500–600	$750–900
H	£600–700	$900–1,050
I	£700–800	$1,050–1,250
J	£800–900	$1,250–1,400
K	£900–1,000	$1,400–1,500
L	£1,000–2,000	$1,500–3,000
M	£2,000–3,000	$3,000–4,500
N	£3,000–4,000	$4,500–6,000
O	£4,000–5,000	$6,000–7,500
P	£5,000–6,000	$7,500–9,000
Q	£6,000–7,000	$9,000–10,700
R	£7,000–8,000	$10,700–12,250
S	£8,000–9,000	$12,250–13,750
T	£9,000–10,000	$13,750–15,000
U	£10,000–15,000	$15,000–23,000
V	£15,000–20,000	$23,000–30,500
W	£20,000–30,000	$30,500–46,000
X	£30,000–40,000	$46,000–61,000
Y	£40,000–50,000	$61,000–76,500
Z	£50,000–60,000	$76,500–92,000
AA	£60,000–70,000	$92,000–107,000
BB	£70,000–80,000	$107,000–122,500
CC	£80,000–90,000	$122,500–138,000
DD	£90,000–100,000	$138,000–153,000
EE	£100,000–150,000	$153,000–230,000
FF	£150,000–200,000	$230,000–305,000
GG	£200,000–250,000	$305,000–385,000
HH	£250,000–300,000	$385,000–460,000
II	£300,000 and over	$460,000 and over

One of Britain's best-known furniture manufacturers, Ercol, was in fact founded by an Italian, Lucian Ercolani in 1920. From his workshop in High Wycombe, Ercolani perfected the technique of steam-bending wood. By the 1950s Ercol had become a household name producing well-designed but unassuming furniture that was affordable. Nest of Tables was designed in 1956 and is just one of several designs that now has iconic status, and is widely regarded as a Mid-Century Modern classic

Foreword

As countries recovered from World War II, designers seized on the new optimism to create ground-breaking styles and products that were unlike anything that had gone before. They were driven by the possibilities of mass production and excited by the host of new materials available to them, many of which had been developed during the war years.

With the rise of youth culture, a market for modern, fashionable goods was born. The younger generation was ready to rebel against social conservatism. While their parents had told them to "sit up straight", the young slouched, and designers were quick to create comfortable chairs over which people could drape themselves. While the older generation was used to having to "make do and mend", the young wholeheartedly embraced the disposable society – they replaced the old with something new and fashionable, a taste epitomized by plastic furniture and paper dresses.

The post-war decades were also characterized by the desire to simplify and modernize the interior by de-cluttering rooms and creating more living space. Separate dining rooms and large entrance halls were deemed unnecessary, resulting in new open-plan layouts, emphasized by sleek structural elements. A new domesticity saw the reinforcement of gender stereotypes after the disruption to the family unit caused by the necessities of war, and young homemakers were enticed by an array of colourful labour-saving devices and bright new abstract patterns. The vogue for entertaining at home led to mass-produced tableware, oven-to-table crockery, and the hostess trolley.

Mid-Century Modern style was for many years derided as being many variations on the theme of kitsch, but the combination of architectural minimalism and organic modernism at its heart has led to its recent re-evaluation. Mid-century classics are enjoying a revival – in fact, many of the most iconic designs have remained in production since they were launched and these continue to inspire the designers of today. This book takes an in-depth look at the artefacts and designers that shaped this important and enduring style.

What came before

Below, left to right: A gilt bronze figural lamp designed by French sculptor François-Raoul Larche, c.1900. It is modelled as the dancer Loïe Fuller, with her diaphanous robes forming the lampshade. 17.5in (44cm) high, **V**

"La Plume", a decorative panel by Alphonse Mucha, shows a woman with jewellery in her hair holding a white feather, with an ornamented halo typical of the Czech artist's work behind her. 29in (72.5cm) high, **Q**

An Arts and Crafts spindled slipper chair by Gustav Stickley. 33in (84cm) high, **H**

Opposite: A William De Morgan ruby lustre charger, highlighted in silver on a cream background. 15in (37cm) wide, **N**

Like most historically significant styles in the decorative arts, Mid-Century Modernism not only evolved from elements of the dominant styles that immediately preceded it, but the movement was also in some respects a reaction against its close antecedents.

The two most fashionable styles of the early 20th century had been Art Nouveau and Arts and Crafts. Largely a European phenomenon, Art Nouveau had emerged initially in France in the late 1880s, at its heart a re-appreciation of the forms of nature. This had been prompted, in part, by a return to "naturalism" in the 19th-century Gothic-Revival style that had preceded it, and also by the imagery employed in contemporary Symbolist art and poetry.

The manner in which Art Nouveau designers and craftsmen represented the forms of nature – primarily plant forms, but also female figures – drew for inspiration on the serpentine lines of 18th-century Rococo decoration, the sinuous interlacings of ancient Celtic ornament, and the asymmetry of recently "rediscovered" traditional Japanese design. A distinctive stylistic fusion, Art Nouveau may have become unfashionable by the outbreak of World War I in 1914, but its emphasis on organic forms was to be picked up again by many members of the Mid-Century Modern movement just 30 or 40 years later.

The Arts and Crafts movement emerged in Britain as early as the 1860s. Better-known in the United States as the Craftsman style, it had a strong following on both sides of the Atlantic by the turn of the 20th century. Enduring well into the 1930s, especially in Britain (albeit in the background), it had started out as a rejection of the historicism and stylistic eclecticism that dominated mass-produced Victorian artefacts.

Rather than a mishmash of poorly reinterpreted earlier styles – notably various revivals of 17th-century Baroque and 18th-century Rococo and Neo-classical styles, sometimes collectively referred to as "Louis Revival" or "Old French" style – the Arts and Crafts advocates wanted something more coherent, honest, and less over-ornamented. For them this translated into the adoption of unpretentious patterns and motifs, primarily flora and fauna with their roots in the medieval English and secularized Gothic vocabularies of ornament. It was, however, the basic philosophy that underpinned this approach – that decoration should be an integral part of a design, rather than a superfluous addition – that was to prove so influential to the ensuing Modern Movement.

The other major Arts and Crafts criticism of late 19th-century historical-revival styles was the generally poor quality of the mass-produced furnishings to which they gave rise. As far as the early proponents of the Arts and Crafts movement (and later purists) were concerned, this called for a return to medieval standards of craftsmanship – in other words, high-quality manufacture carried out by properly trained, skilled hands.

The almost unavoidable result of the handmade approach was higher production costs, which restricted the purchase of such artefacts to the notably wealthier sections of society. However, by the turn of the 20th century some Arts and Crafts designers, especially in the United States, realized that with proper controls in place, more cost-effective, machine-made production techniques and good – or indeed high-quality – products were not necessarily mutually exclusive. Embracing rather than criticizing industrial technology in this way was to pave the way significantly for the acceptance of the Modernist designs that followed.

While Art Nouveau and Arts and Crafts had ushered in the 20th century, the years between the two world wars (1918–39) were dominated by Modernist and Art Deco styles. With its roots in the European ideas of the Vienna Seccession, the Glasgow School, and the Bauhaus, and in the Arts and Crafts-related Mission Style of the United States, Modernism stripped away embellishments ("superfluous trimmings") to make form the object of aesthetic admiration … and form would be determined solely by function.

In practice, this meant for the most part angular, geometric, and unadorned forms, with considerable emphasis placed on the quality and texture of the materials used – notably concrete, chromed tubular steel, and glass. The industrial origins and processes of manufacture were highlighted. Underpinned by a desire to render the home "a machine for living in" – as proposed by of one the movement's leading lights, the architect and designer Le Corbusier – Modernism was exciting, new, and positively futuristic in the 1920s and 1930s. This streamlined, rationalist approach to design also worked well with the severe restrictions, both financial and regarding the availability of materials, of World War II. However, after the privations of the war and the considerable period of austerity that followed, it was perhaps inevitable that Modernism in its pure unornamented form would begin to appear rather boring.

In many respects, the development of a more colourful, flamboyant Mid-Century Modern style as a post-war reaction to what Modernism had become took its cue from the emergence of that other great between-the-wars style: Art Deco. The term

Top: A 1920 mahogany armchair by Emile-Jacques Ruhlmann, known for his beautifully crafted Art Deco furniture and interiors. 38.5in (98cm) high, **V**

Bottom, left to right: A Boch Frères large ovoid vase by Charles Catteau, enamel decorated with antelopes in Persian blue and green crackled glaze. 14in (35.5cm), **L**

A large 1930s Art Deco Daum vase, cased with pale celadon fired enamel over a deep cinnamon ground. 12.5in (32cm) high, **N**

A Clarice Cliff "Red Autumn" square stepped vase, shape 369, hand-painted with a stylized tree and cottage landscape. c.1930. 7.75in (19.5cm) high, **R**

Opposite: A pair of Stuart Art Deco enamelled candleholders, decorated with an abstract geometric pattern of cogs and flashes. 3.25in (8cm) high, **C**

was derived from the *Exposition Internationale des Arts Décoratifs et Industriels Moderne* that had been held in Paris in 1925. Designers took their inspiration from sources as diverse as Léon Bakst's costumes and sets for the Ballets Russes, the art movements of Expressionism, Cubism, and Futurism, and, following the excavation of Tutankhamun's tomb and the discovery of Aztec temples in the early 1920s, ancient Egyptian and native Central American art. The result was a range of exciting "new" decorative imagery rendered in bright colours for the Jazz Age, standing in marked contrast to the horrors of World War I and the financial hardships that had followed.

However, the parallels between Art Deco and Mid-Century Modern styles are essentially confined to the nature of their emergence in reaction to world events. As Art Deco developed during the 1930s, the forms and decorative imagery associated with the style became increasingly geometrical, abstract, and vigorously streamlined. In other words, it became more overtly Modernist and in doing so displayed characteristics that, according to the influential French designer Paul Iribe, involved "sacrificing the flower on the altar of the machine" – a sacrifice that Mid-Century Modern style, with its notable revival of all things organic, was about to remedy.

The New Look

Inevitably, World War II (1939–45) had an adverse effect on the decorative arts. In many countries, raw materials, especially metals and timber, were prioritized for use in the war effort, while numerous manufacturing facilities were adapted and diverted to military production. Moreover, although the extensive destruction caused by bombing raids led to considerable need in many parts of Europe, the majority of people could ill afford new furnishings, let alone other decorative artefacts, even when they were available.

The economic up-turn upon which a revival in both the production and consumption of the decorative arts was ultimately dependent began in the United States, the country with the largest economy and, significantly, one of the few that had escaped invasion and bombing. As the post-war American economy accelerated to record-breaking levels of productivity in a relatively short time, it became possible for the United States to export some of this momentum to kick-start overseas markets. Between April 1948 and December 1951, about $100 billion dollars in today's money was pumped into Europe via the European Recovery Program, better known as the Marshall Plan, with the upshot that by 1951 the economies of almost all the countries that had joined the OEEC (Organisation for European Economic Co-operation) had been rebuilt to their pre-war levels and beyond.

With the financial wherewithal to both produce and purchase gradually restored, what would designers want to design after the trauma of the war years? And, just as significantly, what would consumers want to buy? Although it took place in the relatively exclusive world of *haute couture* fashion, much of the initial essence or spirit of post-World War II design was encapsulated in the spring 1947 collection of French couturier Christian Dior (1905–57) – aptly labelled by *Harper's Bazaar* as the "New Look". Characterized by an extravagant use of extravagant fabrics, it was a refreshing and glamorous antidote to wartime and post-war austerity. Dior's designs also marked a return to a notably curvaceous, more overtly feminine look (a flatter, more linear style having generally been in vogue since the appearance of the "flapper" dresses of the 1920s). Gradually rippling down and out from the heights of *haute couture* to what we would now call high-street fashion, the hugely influential "New Look" also had its counterparts in many other areas of post-war design.

The prevailing styles of the 1930s had been Modernism and Art Deco. Originally seen by many as pleasingly rational, dynamic, and futuristic, the unornamented "form-follows-function" rationale of the former and the geometric shapes of the latter had begun to appear rather too severe to many war-jaundiced eyes. In Britain in particular, this development may well have been exacerbated by the government-sponsored introduction in 1942 of "utility furniture". Like many other goods at the time, new furniture was rationed; reserved for newly-weds and people whose homes had been bombed. Designed by the expert members of the Advisory Committee on Utility Furniture to make the best use of scarce timber, the furniture was constructed in the traditions of the Arts and Crafts Movement, but was exceptionally severe in its simplicity of form and lack of ornamentation. Basically, it was time – and not just in Britain – for something a bit less linear, a bit more curvaceous, and certainly more ornamented and colourful.

The decorative style that developed after the war, dominated the 1950s, and endured into the early 1970s has become known as "Mid-Century Modern". In fact, there had already been an inkling of it in embryonic form as early as the 1930s, a decade in which some Scandinavian designers had developed a quite distinctive, rounded style of furniture subsequently known as "Soft Modernism". While adhering to the basic simplicity of line and form of Modernist furniture, these designers rejected the "coldness" of the materials of mass production, such as steel and plastic, from which much of it was made. As the Finnish designer Alvar Aalto (1898–1976) observed, in this respect Modernist furniture was "unsatisfactory from a human point of view". Instead, Aalto and other Scandinavian designers such as Bruno Mathsson chose to use natural materials – most notably wood – in less machine-like and more organic, sculptural forms.

Opposite: Part of Christian Dior's spring 1947 collection, the "Bar" suit epitomizes fashion's "New Look", with its wasp-waisted silk shantung jacket and full skirt in wool crêpe.

Below: Designed by Charles and Ray Eames, the moulded plywood and leather lounge chair and ottoman were launched by Hermann Miller in 1956 and are still in production today. Chair 32in (81cm) high, **M**

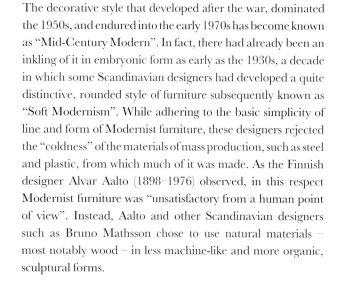

In the early 1940s and on the other side of the Atlantic, the Scandinavian promotion of wood in this context was given a further and significant boost by the American designers Charles Eames (1907–78) and his wife, Ray (1912–88). The Eameses developed a method for moulding bonded plywood in more than one direction – a technique which, when adapted to industrial production, allowed them to create a host of innovative furniture designs after the war and throughout the 1950s (see pages 38-101).

The wartime and post-war development of new techniques for working materials was, however, by no means confined to wood. Throughout the war military designers, especially in the aircraft industry, had pioneered the use of a number of new materials and techniques that were to give the decorative arts designers of the 1950s much greater freedom. For example, lightweight but relatively strong and durable materials such as aluminium increasingly featured in furniture construction, as did thinner and lighter steel. The latter inspired the creation of lightweight wire-rod furniture by designers such as Harry Bertoia (1915–78) and Warren Platner (1919–2006).

Other innovations that were to have a profound effect on furniture design included new forms of upholstery. Notable among these were a type of rubber padding developed by Italian tyre manufactures and, from Scandinavia, foam padding made from polystyrene beads that could be steamed into just about any desired shape. Applied over an almost equally mouldable fibreglass frame, this foam padding made it possible to produce curvaceous, streamlined, and sculptural forms, such as the now-iconic "Swan" and "Egg" chairs by Danish designer Arne Jacobsen (1902–71). Of course, such padding could also be applied over sheet metal – an application that softened and eased, both literally and symbolically, the inherent coldness and, according to the complaints of the Scandinavian Soft Modernists, "unwelcoming" qualities of that material.

Perhaps the most important development in new materials and techniques derived from the greater affordability of petroleum-based plastics as a result of an oil glut in the 1950s and 1960s. Combined with new injection-moulding techniques, this allowed designers to fully exploit plastic's ability to retain almost any form and, just as significantly, take advantage of the fact that it could produced in a kaleidoscope of colours.

The growing popularity of colourful plastics at this time can be gauged not only by their increased use in the manufacture of furniture and numerous other domestic artefacts, such as light fittings and tableware, but also by the fact that some objects not even made from plastic, such as the glass "Carnaby" vases

Left: A clear glass vase with murrines and cane inserts, designed by Ansolo Fuga for A.Ve.M., Murano, in c.1958. 9.75in (25cm) high, **M**

Right: A red and white cased glass "Carnaby" vase designed by Per Lutken for Holmegaard in 1961. This range was deliberately designed to resemble plastic. 8.75in (22cm) high, **D**

produced by Danish glassmaker Per Lütken (1916–98) in the 1960s, were designed to look as if they had been.

After decades of artistic stagnation, innovative glass making enjoyed a resurgence on the Venetian island of Murano from the late 1940s onwards. Local glassmakers collaborated with international artists who had trained as painters and sculptors, thereby revolutionizing Italian glass design. Traditional techniques were revived to create a "new look". Murrines, small coloured tesserae used to decorate the surface of a piece of glass, were now produced in modern colour combinations that expressed post-war exuberance.

In addition to making much greater use of colour and creating more sculptural forms than their Modernist predecessors, the Mid-Century Modernists also revived, to varying degrees, the use of decorative pattern. Many of the patterns that became fashionable were, like the curvaceous shapes they employed, inspired by nature, and in that respect the Mid-Century Modernists had much in common with their Art Nouveau predecessors of the late 19th and early 20th century. One important difference, however, was that many of the natural forms that inspired designers the mid-20th century had never been seen prior to the development of powerful electron microscopes. Of these many newly discovered microscopic forms, which included the surprisingly symmetrical crystalline-like composition snowflakes, the asymmetrical amoeba provided the greatest source of inspiration. Much evident in contemporary art, for exmple in the paintings of Salvador Dalí (1904–89) and Joan Miró (1893–1983), amoeboid-shaped motifs became particularly prevalent in patterns applied to wallpaper, furnishing fabrics, ceramics, and glass.

This new microscopic natural imagery, sometimes referred to as "Organic Modernism", was the product of a technological development. In that respect it had its counterpart in the "Space Age" imagery that also proved popular from the late 1950s onwards – notable examples include table lamps in the form of rockets and ceiling pendants in shape of flying saucers – as the technological push to put man into space gathered momentum and increasingly captured the public imagination.

Midwinter Primavera

A rare Midwinter "Fashion"-shape TV plate, printed and hand-painted with the "Primavera" pattern. 12.5in (32cm) diam, **B**

The "Primavera" pattern designed by Jessie Tait (1928–2010) was initially unpopular with the public when it was introduced in 1954. Its popularity increased only after the London department store Heal's began to stock wares with this design. Combining the popular 1950s pattern of polka dots with amoeba-like and organic shapes, the example shown above is a variation of the original version of the design used on the "Stylecraft" range of shapes.

The TV plate, with its recessed sections for different foods, is a relatively rare shape. Its existence reflects dramatic changes in contemporary society. The Queen's Coronation in 1953 had led to a huge growth of sales of home television sets in Britain and, following the establishment of ITV in 1955, more and more British people were turning to the television as their main source of home entertainment. Similar developments emerged worldwide heralding a new way of spending leisure time in the home, with electronic colour sets emerging in the US in the mid-1950s. This in turn led to the development of specially designed tableware and furniture.

Historical precedent demonstrates that the taste of the general public is, at almost any given time, far less adventurous than that of a small design-aware elite. But following the widespread trauma of World War II, people in many countries really did appear to want a "new look". Reinforcing this desire was a post-war growth in communications. Events such as the Good Design exhibition initiated by the Museum of Modern Art in New York in 1950, the Festival of Britain held in 1951, and subsequent similar exhibitions that took place in many European cities throughout the 1950s, promoted the new designs of the Mid-Century Modernists in a traditional manner. However, combined with advertising (both direct and in the form of product placement), the new medium of television began to bring the prospect of these exciting new products right into people's homes, initially in the United States and later in Europe. Moreover, as the post-war population, and with it suburbia, boomed, the demand for enticing new and well-designed furnishings, tableware, and all manner of appliances mushroomed accordingly.

This consumer boom was further reinforced by another significant social development: the post-war growth of a youth culture ready to rebel against political, social, and artistic conservatism and the older generation's philosophy of "make do and mend". On a tide of brash, colourful Pop art and loud rock and roll, the balance of power inexorably shifted in favour of a new, forward-looking generation and the designs and products of the Mid-Century Modernists benefited as a result. Yet by the mid-1960s, Mid-Century Modernism would, ironically, begin to be supplanted by aspects of the very youth culture that had helped fuel it: as a reflection of an ever-increasing rejection of traditional institutions, designs in the decorative arts were to become, under the banner of "Anti-Design", more and more extreme. Rejecting almost everything the Mid-Century Modernists had stood for, the Post-Modernists were about to come into their own … but that, as they say, is another story.

Interiors

Introduction

One of the most significant developments in architecture and interior design in the mid-20th century, under the aegis of the Modern and then the Mid-Century Modern movements, was a renewed emphasis on the home as an integrated whole. The building's exterior, and often what was around it, had a major impact on the interior, not only on the way it was structurally divided, but critically, also on what it looked and felt like. Probably the last time such attention was paid to exploiting what was outside to enhance what was inside was in the 18th century, when the great landscape architect Capability Brown "judiciously manipulated the components of nature" to provide wonderful vistas for the privileged occupants of some of the grandest country houses in Britain.

The "re-discovery" of nature and its integration with exterior and interior design by pioneering 20th-century architects such as Frank Lloyd Wright (1867–1959) may have been in the tradition of Brown, but its more immediate inspiration lay in the re-appreciation of organic forms by the Art Nouveau movement of the late 19th and early 20th century, and in the belief of advocates of the Arts and Crafts movement that decorative effects should be an integral part of the design, rather than an add-on. In part it was also a reaction to the manner in which Modernism, in its purist "form-follows-function" guise, had often dispensed with ornamentation altogether.

Left: Fallingwater was designed by Frank Lloyd Wright in 1935 as a weekend retreat for the Kaufmann family of Pittsburgh. It is dramatically located over the Bear Run waterfalls in rural south-western Pennsylvania, USA.

Below: A Japanese influence is evident in the Fallingwater interiors, not only in the low tables and seating but also in the rooms' visual integration with the natural surroundings.

One interesting consequence of this mid-century integration of nature in architectural design was the breakdown of the almost monopolistic influence that urban living had come to exert on innovative décor. Architects and designers such as Wright, Ludwig Mies van der Rohe (1886–1969), Jean Prouvé (1901–84), Richard Neutra (1892–1970), Pierre Koenig (1925–2004), Charles Eames (1907–78), Arne Jacobsen (1902–71), and Eero Saarinen (1910–61) now conceived residential architecture and interiors that could just as easily integrate into a cityscape as sit comfortably against a rural backdrop.

The primary means of bringing the outside in was the use of glass in the form of "picture windows", with improved manufacturing techniques making ever larger examples possible. This is not to say, however, that greater size equated to uniformity: most of the long windows in Wright's iconic Fallingwater, the house he designed in 1935 for the Kaufmann family in Mill Run, Pennsylvania, are significantly narrower than the much taller picture windows in, for example, Prouvé's almost equally iconic "pre-fabricated" home near Nancy, in the Lorraine region of France. Both allow the occupants spectacular views of the surrounding countryside, making it a significant component of the interior décor, but Wright's windows generally created a darker interior than Prouvé's.

In many respects this issue of natural light is indicative of a major trend: in contrast to their dark 1930s predecessors, such as those in Wright's buildings, Mid-Century Modern interiors become lighter and lighter after World War II, as can be seen in the large-windowed homes of influential architects and designers such as Koenig, Saarinen, and the Eameses. Just as important in conveying the style beyond the design cognoscenti to the general public is the light-and-airy quality emphasized in contemporary promotional shots of their work. As a psychological reaction to the "dark days" of the war, the appeal to the public at large of Mid-Century Modernism's "let there be light" approach is readily understandable, and of course a greater ingress of natural light was augmented by increasingly sophisticated electric lighting inside – at ceiling, floor, tabletop, and work-surface levels.

In addition to using large expanses of glass, there were other ways of breaking the "barrier" between what was inside and what was outside. For example, the Mid-Century Modernists

A group of "Cité" armchairs (1930) in the home of their creator, the French designer Jean Prouvé. The room is notable for its floor-to-ceiling windows and views over the surrounding countryside. Incorporating coated sheet steel rockers, the chairs are still in production today with Vitra.

made increasing use of tall, sliding glass doors, while in locations with suitably temperate climates, most notably California, outdoor "rooms" open to the elements on one, two, or three sides became fashionable. These had plenty of historical precedent in the cloisters and covered walkways of Medieval European monasteries. Japanese architecture inspired the incorporation of elemental nature within the building itself, such as Wright's inclusion in Fallingwater of a spring, a stream, and rock from the waterfall below the house.

The more conventional way of linking the exterior to the interior was to make overt use in the latter of materials usually associated with the former, chief among them wood and stone. Whether in the form of slabs of limestone, granite, or marble, or a composite material such as terrazzo (a poured-on aggregate of stone and glass chips), stone floors proved equally suitable for indoor living areas as for exterior terraces, and were particularly popular in Mid-Century Modern houses in North America. Contrasting-textured stone finishes or ceramic tiles were also usually employed on, in, and around hearths, and often on walls as well. By way of pleasing contrast, tongue-and-groove wooden panelling was frequently the favoured material for ceilings in such interiors, especially on the west coast of the United States and in Scandinavia.

In both those locations wood was easily available, and so it is not surprising that when they were not using stone or tile on the floor, architects and interior designers often chose wood instead, particularly in Scandinavia. The wide variety of woods on offer – from softwoods such as pine and cedar to hardwoods such as oak, beech, and mahogany – meant a huge palette of colour options, from blonde through yellows and browns to red, especially if the wood was treated with stains or varnishes. Moreover, whether it is used on floors or ceilings, laid in broad panels or narrower tongue-and-groove planks, wood invariably conveys a sense of warmth – especially when contrasted with stone or tile. At the same time, it satisfies the Mid-Century Modernists' desire for a clean, crisp rectilinear quality in the basic architectural fixtures and fittings – a

Top: Charles and Ray Eames
in their home in Pacific Palisades,
Los Angeles. Their iconic black leather "Eames Lounge Chair"
and "Ottoman" (1956) are still in production.

Bottom: The distinctive form of Eero Sarinen's "Tulip" chair
(1956), made of aluminium, fibreglass, and plastic, is both
organic and futuristic, anticipating the Space Age.

Opposite: A classic mid-century modern chair – the triangular
plastic, steel, and foam "Coconut" (George Nelson, 1955) – sits
happily with an earlier Modernist icon, the chromed steel and
leather "Barcelona" (Mies van der Rohe and Lilly Reich, 1929).

quality also much in evidence when wood was deployed in the construction of the vertebrae-like, open-plan staircases that featured in many Mid-Century Modern builds. (A similar organic warmth, as well as a grid-like look, was also provided by cork tiles, which were sometimes used in lieu of wood.)

Wood, that most traditional of materials, also featured in much of the fashionable furniture of the period. Favoured by the Scandinavians, notably designers such as Alvar Aalto (1898–1976) and Bruno Mathsson (1907–88), who considered it a "far more satisfactory material from a human point of view" than cold steel, wood was also given a new lease of life for furniture construction in the United States following the development of a new technique for moulding bonded plywood by American designers Charles and Ray Eames. This new method allowed for more organic, sculptural shapes to be produced, and thereby tapped into the Mid-Century Modern desire for more natural forms.

Other traditional materials the Mid-Century Modernists employed to make their interiors softer – and more overtly decorative – than those of their starker Modernist predecessors were wallpaper and fabrics. Being derived from wood pulp, wallpaper fulfilled the "organic material" agenda, but far more importantly it provided a means for displaying colour and pattern. Prominent among the latter were organic motifs, such as amoeba-like forms (see "The New Look", pages 16-23). Equally prevalent, however, was imagery either taken from or in the style of contemporary art. Indeed, the Mid-Modernist fashion for applying wallpaper only to a single "feature wall" gave the imagery portrayed on it a far more focused, picture-like status than it would have had if applied all around the

Right: In his 1946 design for the Kaufmann Desert House in Palm Springs, California, Richard Neutra struck a balance between emphasizing a strong connection to the surrounding desert landscape at the same time as providing shelter from its often harsh climate.

Below: Designed by Pierre Koenig in 1957, Case Study House No. 21 is located in a canyon in the Hollywood Hills, Los Angeles. In this building, also known as the Bailey House, Koenig created a truly open-plan design sympathetically linked to its exterior by capitalizing on the huge spans possible with lightweight steel-frame construction techniques.

Left: The Homewood, designed in 1938 by British architect Patrick Gwynne at age 24 for his parents and built in Esher, Surrey. Strongly influenced by Le Corbusier's Villa Savoye in the outskirts of Paris and Mies van der Rohe's Tugendhat House in Brno, Czech Republic, its design has been described as "an ingenious adaptation to site and prospect".

Below: Looking out over the desert landscape of Palm Springs, from a bedroom in the Richard Neutra-designed Kaufmann House.

room. Many of the fabrics employed for soft furnishings, from rugs and carpets to upholstery, cushion covers, and curtains became, if anything, even more like fine-art than wallpaper in their design and status, and did even more to soften, colour, brighten up and – very importantly – personalize mid-century interiors (see "Textiles", pages 184-193).

All of this is not to say that some of the "colder", intrinsically less decorative materials favoured by the early Modernists disappeared from Mid-Century Modern interiors – far from it. Lightweight but sturdy aluminium was often used for large window frames, as well as in some furniture construction. Steel also retained much of its popularity from earlier in the 20th century, not only in its role as a structural architectural support, but also as a featured component of many innovative chair designs. Moreover, the presence of steel in seating wasn't just confined to new furniture – many earlier Modernist pieces, such as the "Barcelona" chair designed by Mies van der Rohe in 1929 kept reappearing in post-war interiors, and by the middle of the century, they were well on their way to acquiring the iconic status they have today. Increasingly sophisticated man-made plastics also began to feature more freqently in the mid-century home. They were far removed from "natural" organic materials, but their strength and mouldability enabled designers to create overtly organic shapes – Saarinen's classic "Tulip" chairs and tables being particularly notable examples. The designer's almost

Art Nouveau-like use of sweeping organic forms is in many respects even more overtly evident in his iconic TWA Flight Center, opened in 1962 at New York's Idlewild Airport, which was renamed in honour of John F. Kennedy in 1963.

Of course, plastics and metals also played a less glamorous but no less vital role in the new labour-saving household appliances that emerged in the post-war prosperity of the 1950s and 1960s. The Mid-Century Modern architects and designers may have revived the forms of nature and brought them inside, but in many respects Le Corbusier's early Modernist vision of the home as "a machine for living in" still held good. Indeed, it could be argued that one of the chief successes of the Mid-Century Modernists was to have softened that machine, to have made it appear more natural, more organic, and ultimately more human.

Right and below: The exterior of the TWA Flight Center designed by Eero Saarinen resembled a huge bird, its wings spread in flight. The ergonomically efficient interior was equally "organic", with undulating levels and sweeping curves.

Furniture and lighting

Introduction

A George Nelson "Coconut" chair, designed 1955 for Herman Miller, upholstered in royal blue vinyl, 41.5in (105cm) wide, **M**

The term 'Mid-Century Modern' might sound a little like a contemporary attempt to categorize a style currently popular with interior decorators and designers, but it's not a new label. Largely used to describe developments in architecture and design, it strives to define a period of innovation and advancement that roughly falls between the mid 1930s and the late1960s. Dating back to the 1950s, it is a label that requires some leeway; a stricter definition would limit the understanding of the important influences that preceded the acceptance of Mid-Century Modernism as a design genre.

The recurring motif in the evolution of the Mid-Century Modern style seems to have been human strife and war. Throughout the course of the 20th century, it is impossible to separate developments in the field of design from the socio-economic sufferings of a war-torn world – this period in history is defined by traumatic, tumultuous events.

World War I had already reshaped the social and economic structure of Europe. For a whole generation, the rise of the Machine Age and the slaughter in the trenches had brought about a shift in the psyche. Gone was the flamboyance of Art Nouveau; instead the Dutch De Stijl movement (founded in 1917) and the Bauhaus school in Germany (founded in 1919) challenged established schools of thought, building on the ideas of the pre-war avant-garde to further the ideals of Modernism. This was "shock" progress based on a rejection of everything previous generations held dear. It's a taste that defined the 1920s while at the same time providing a strong foundation for the designers that would go on to produce the iconic products of the Mid-Century Modern movement, as well as influencing and teaching the design stars of the future.

The surface glamour of the inter-war period belied a general political unease, with Europe on an inexorable march towards the horror of World War II. These years were a rich period of experimentation, particularly in the field of furniture design, when designers such as Marcel Breuer (1902–81), Charlotte Perriand (1903–99), Jean Prouvé (1901–84), and Gio Ponti (1891–1979) set the pace in utilizing new materials and mass-production techniques, and developed radical ideas to further the cause of design.

There is a general misconception that World War II was a dry period for design, but it would be untrue to think that things stood still. In the United States, the Mid-Century Modern movement was already well established, with ground-breaking innovators such as George Nelson (1908–86), Charles (1907–78) and Ray Eames (1912–88), and Hans (1914–55) and Florence Knoll (b. 1917) designing what would become the defining furniture, dwellings, and accessories of the 20th century. At the same time, American companies were also nurturing a raft of cosmopolitan design talent that had arrived from Europe before the outbreak of war. It was in the United States that the ideals of Mid-Century Modernism were almost seamlessly absorbed into society, producing a looser, more organic form of the style that was anchored in the residential sector. The "post and beam" method of construction made possible the light and airy suburbs of a burgeoning post-war American boom, and this move towards spacious, uncluttered interiors was popularly known as the "California Modern" style.

The post-war revitalization of Europe was of paramount importance. The construction of affordable housing for the millions of displaced people called for radical ideas based on fast, efficient mass-production techniques; affordable furniture and consumer goods were also required. Supported by the Marshall Plan, the shattered economies of Europe quickly grew on the wave of post-war reconstruction and consumerism. Material shortages pushed designers into new avenues of thought; construction techniques pioneered for military use found different applications in

Top: A pair of ceiling lamps designed by Serge Mouille in 1950, aluminum with black exteriors and reflective white interiors. 62in (158cm) long, **T**

Below left: A red "Little Tulip" armchair on a tubular swivel chrome base, designed by Pierre Paulin for Artifort in 1965 with clean, ergonomic lines; said to be "one of the most comfortable chairs ever made". 29in (74cm) high, **G**

Below right: A late 1950s teak cabinet designed by Hans Wegner for Ry Mobler, with two sliding doors over an arrangement of four drawers in two rows. 62.26in (158cm) wide, **L**

the civilian world. By the 1950s, this period of increased prosperity and high employment, coupled with a new-found optimism, was beginning to fill homes with good design.

In the United Kingdom, where the enforced frugality of post-war rationing was coming to an end, the 1951 Festival of Britain showcased the best of British, providing the perfect platform for the new design talent of future luminaries such as Robin (1915–2010) and Lucienne Day (1917–2010), and Ernest Race (1913–64). The exhibition attracted more than ten million visitors, and London's South Bank became synonymous with the idea of Britain's post-war recovery.

Experimentation with modern materials challenged the artisanal ideals of European craft-based design. The use of lightweight metals, steel rods, fibreglass, and petroleum-based plastics revolutionized the form of furniture, and despite the ever-present natural Scandinavian aesthetic, Danish designers such as Arne Jacobsen (1902–71) and Verner Panton (1926–98) were among the first to fully embrace the possibilities these new materials afforded. Jacobsen's sculptural, upholstered "Egg" and "Swan" lounge chairs, both designed in 1958

for the Royal Hotel in Copenhagen, stand testament to this. Similarly, Panton explored radical shapes using fabric-covered sheet metal, wire frames, and moulded plastics. His revolutionary injection-moulded "Panton" chair (1959–60) is an enduring classic.

Modern materials were not exclusive to furniture production. Architects and product designers also readily embraced their versatility to provide complete interior design solutions, including lighting. Plastics were perfect for sculptural forms, and Italian designers excelled in this field – the fabulous see-through "Acrilica" table lamp (1962) designed by Joe Colombo (1930–71) is a masterpiece. Danish manufacturer Louis Poulsen Lighting collaborated on many 20th-century classics, including the "Artichoke" lamp designed by Poul Henningsen (1894–1967) in 1958 and Verner Panton's "Panthella" (1971), and continues to work with eminent designers today.

Mid-Century Modern has seen a massive resurgence in recent years, strongly influencing everything from clothing to trends in home decoration. "Retro" elements are frequently seen infiltrating advertising, film, television, and interiors. While purists strive to obtain "the look" using authentic period pieces, the market is strong for classics that have remained in continuous production and sit easily with contemporary styles.

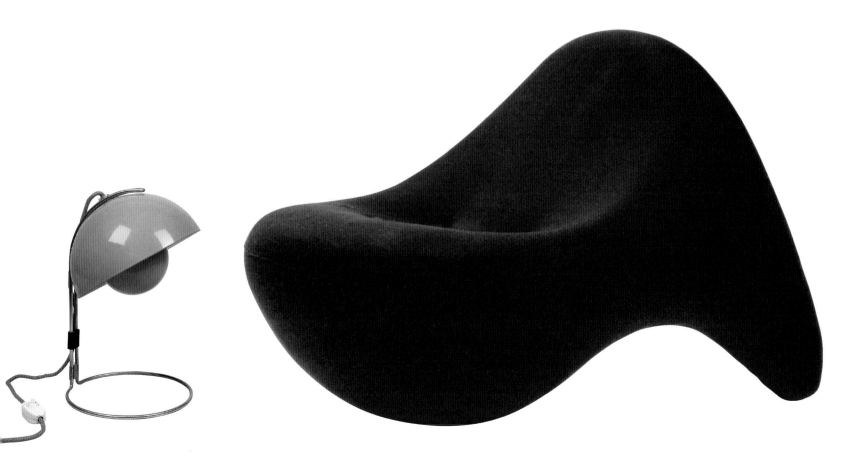

Left: A "Reale" table with a plate-glass top on a complex varnished cherry wood base, desgined by Carlo Mollino in 1946. 63in (72cm) wide, **W**

Below: Three 1950s beech and elm Ercol spindle back kitchen chairs. 35 in (89cm) high, **C**

Scandinavia

Scandinavian design was without doubt the epitome of post-war "good taste". The cabinetmaker's tradition remained central to the whole concept of practical pieces that relied on the age-old skills of the craftsman and natural materials for their undeniably Scandinavian look. The Nordic tradition is rooted in centuries of rural-based culture, as opposed to the urban/industrial model of other parts of Europe. Given the sometimes turbulent political histories of Denmark, Sweden, Finland, Norway, and Iceland, it is interesting that these countries have such a cohesive design identity, as exemplified by the work of Danish designer Finn Juhl (1912–89). His "Chieftain" chair (1949) is a sculptural rosewood and leather classic, which was executed by master craftsman Niels Vodder.

The post-war period required a new direction. Relative isolation during the war had hampered the flow of new ideas from America and the rest of Europe, and Scandinavian designers were faced with the challenge of moving away from the tradition of small workshops into a more innovative period of mass production without sacrificing any of the ideals intrinsic to Scandinavian style. The creation of functional classics using innovative materials became central to the approach of the men and women who shaped the direction of Modern Scandinavian design, while protecting the deep-rooted Nordic quality that so defines their work. From the sculptural forms created by Juhl to the mass-produced "Ant" chair (1951–2) by Arne Jacobsen (1902–71), it was an aesthetic that went on to dominate international design.

Earlier influences fostered by Eliel Saarinen (1873–1950), the Finnish architect who designed and headed the Cranbrook Academy of Art in Michigan in the early 1930s, had been crucial to American interest in Scandinavian design. The Finnish pavilion designed by Alvar Aalto (1898–1976) and the concept of "Swedish Modern" had been great successes at the New York World's Fair of 1939, and this interest was rejuvenated after the war. In 1954, the Design in Scandinavia exhibition, which promoted a Scandinavian way of living in every medium from glass to furniture, embarked on a tour of the US and Canada lasting three-and-a-half years.

This is a period that is hugely popular with decorators and collectors today. Furniture designers such as Hans Wegner (1914–2007), Ole Wanscher (1903–85), and his mentor Kaare Klint (1888–1954), emphasized the Danish cabinet-making tradition while creating functional and highly sculptural classics. Børge Mogensen (1914–72) had also worked closely with Klint to produce simple, dependable, but beautifully made pieces, which helped Danish design gain worldwide respect. Poul Kjærholm (1929–80) pursued new avenues in Scandinavian design with elegantly framed metal furniture more reminiscent of the Modern movement. His "PK22" chair (1955–6) has achieved iconic status and is still in production today. Finnish designers such as Ilmari Tapiovaara (1914–99) and Yrjö Kukkapuro (b. 1933) similarly challenged the Nordic tradition to produce the kind of furniture often labelled as "Scandinavian Functionalist".

Kjærholm, Mogensen, Wegner

Scandinavian design has its roots in a strong cultural and historic philosophy based on craftsmanship and tradition. After World War II, a new generation of designers built on this tradition while also addressing the need to adapt these principles of good craftsmanship to new industrial production methods. The sculptural, elegant wooden furniture produced by Danish designers such as Hans Wegner (1914–2007) and Børge Mogensen (1914–72), both from the cabinet-making tradition, had a more human, gentler feel than the cold, metallic austerity of pre-war Modern design. These designers worked primarily with traditional, rather than cutting-edge, manufacturing techniques. In 1983, Wegner said: "Technically there was nothing new in our work.".

A daybed in white oak designed by Børge Mogensen and manufactured by Erhard Rasmussen, with an Erhard Rasmussen label. 76.5in (194cm) long, **M**

An oak credenza designed by Hans Wegner for R.Y. Mobler, with sliding caned-front doors and aluminum legs with rosewood tipped feet, with branded mark. 78.75in (200cm) wide, **N**

Danish designers of the period made a lot furniture from natural materials. This chair, probably by Børge Mogensen also evokes the "Peacock" chair by fellow Danish designer Hans Wegner. 37.25in (93cm) high, **K**

A "Papa Bear" teak armchair designed in 1951 by Hans Wegner for A. P. Stolen. Known as the Teddy Bear chair. Upholstered in beige wool with stamped mark. 39in (99cm) high, **R**

Poul Kjærholm

A "PK-33" stool, designed by Poul Kjærholm for Fritz Hansen in 1959. Chromium plated steel and plywood with a leather cushion. 14in (35.5cm) high, **M**

Poul Kjærholm (1929–80) graduated from the Copenhagen School of Arts and Crafts in 1952. Kjærholm's work is characterized by its understated sophistication, grace, clean lines, and attention to detail. He managed to combine the typically Scandinavian skill of imbuing furniture with warmth and humanity with the more rigorous, purist approach of the German Bauhaus. Although he always considered functionality an unconditional requirement, he was also reluctant to compromise himself as an artist. While most of his contemporaries chose wood as their primary material, Kjærholm preferred steel, using it in combination with materials such as wood, leather, cane, or marble.

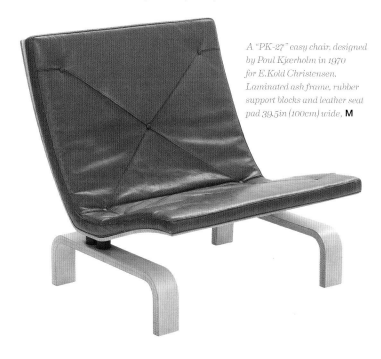

A "PK-27" easy chair, designed by Poul Kjærholm in 1970 for E.Kold Christensen. Laminated ash frame, rubber support blocks and leather seat pad 39.5in (100cm) wide, **M**

Verner Panton

(1926-1998)

Top: A Verner Panton "Ball" chandelier, designed for J.Luber, in polished chrome and brushed brass. 39in (97.5cm) high, **S**

Below left: "Pantella" desklight, c1970 designed by Verner Panton for Louis Poulsen. 28in (71cm) high, **E**

Below right: "Heart" chair, by Verner Panton, upholstered in original red fabric. 40in (101.5cm) high, **M**

Denmark was the centre of the post-war design boom of the 1950s. Struggling in its midst was the young architect and designer Verner Panton. He started his career in the architectural practice of Arne Jacobsen, where he worked from 1950 to 1952, learning a gread deal. As much artist as architect, Panton went on to buck the natural, organic trends followed by his fellow Danish designers to produce bolder, more industrial pieces, experimenting with man-made materials such as plastics. He set out across Europe in his customized Volkswagen camper van, hoping to peddle his innovative style to manufacturers and distributors. Panton got his big break with the "Cone" chair (1958). Originally designed for his parents' guesthouse, the Kom-igen (Danish for "come again") inn on the island of Funen, it was featured in a shoot for the design magazine *Mobilia* surrounded by naked mannequins. The photograph caused a scandal, but helped Panton establish himself as an exponent of Pop culture.

Panton's repertoire was diverse, ranging from lamps and textiles to furniture. Other career milestones include the "Heart" chair (1959) and the iconic "Panton" chair (1967). The world's first plastic cantilever seat moulded in a single piece, this sleek, stackable technical masterpiece has come to symbolize Panton's flair. The "Living Tower" (1968–9) epitomizes his playfulness: this combination of unique shapes, bold colours, and innovative materials singles out Panton as a design visionary of the 20th century.

The "Living Tower",
designed by Verner Panton
for Vitra AG in 1968/9.
78.75in (200cm) wide

Soft Modernism

In the 1950s and 1960s, Scandinavian design was considered the epitome of "good taste" by the style-conscious public in both Europe and the United States. At this time, a new generation of Scandinavian designers took the clean lines of the Modern movement and united them with the softer, more traditional properties of wood and leather. The resulting furniture is strikingly modern but also comfortably familiar.

Hans Olsen (1919–92), who studied under Kaare Klint at the Royal Danish Academy's Furniture School from 1941 to 1943, experimented with form and materials. One of Olsen's most influential designs was the "Bikini" chair, designed in 1961.

Other designers such as Jørgen Høvelskov (1935–2005) from Denmark looked to the past for inspiration. Høvelskov's "Harp" chair from 1968 is based on a Viking ship's bow section, and the configuration of the seat gives the design a powerful visual identity. The chair is a sculptural object, but also strangely comfortable to sit in.

Above: A solid rosewood settee upholstered in olive green leather, model no.800, designed by Hans Olsen in 1956 for Chr. Sörensen & Co, Denmark, brand: C/S Made in Denmark and Danish assay mark. 69in (175cm) wide, **N**

Below: A set of six Danish teak and leather chairs designed by Ejvind Johansson in 1961 for Gern Møbelfabrik. 30in (76cm) high, **O**

Left: A Jørgen Høvelskov "Harp" chair, designed 1968, manufactured by Christensen and Larsen, the ebonised frame with synthetic string "flag". **J**

A Danish teak oval articulated dining table, designed in 1959 by Peter Hvidt and Orla Molgaard-Nielsen for France and Son. 28.75in (73cm) high, **O**

A Hans Olsen teak "Bikin" chair, c. 1961. 29.5in (75cm) **L**

Upholstered in leather, the "Karuselli" armchair (c.1965) by Finnish designer Yrjö Kukkapuro (b. 1933) mounts a clear but innovative challenge to the world of Scandinavian design. Designed in 1965, the chair owes its name, which means "carousel" in Finnish, to the way it swivels and rocks. Legend has it that the chair was inspired by Kukkapuro falling asleep in the snow after a particularly drunken party and realizing that the impression left behind was ideally suited to a chair embracing the human form. "A chair should be softly shaped as people are," Kukkapuro once said, "and if at all possible just as beautiful."

Quistgaard, Tapiovaara, Visser, Wanscher, Winblad

Some Scandinavian designers were very much influenced by past furniture styles, such as Ole Wanscher (1903–85). A student of Kaare Klint, he eventually took over Klint's job at the Royal Danish Academy and went on to write extensively about subjects such as "Furniture Types" and the "History of the Art of Furniture".

An influential Finnish designer was Ilmari Tapiovaara (1914–99), who originally trained as an interior architect. Many of Tapiovaara's designs were a modern interpretation of historical ones, and it is interesting to note that he was one of the few Scandinavian designers who applied himself to designing low-cost standardized furniture. In the late 1930s and early 1940s, Tapiovaara worked as artistic director for Finnish furniture manufacturers Asko Oy and Keravan Puuteollisuus. Between 1946 and 1947, he and his wife Annikki designed furniture for a new student-housing complex in Helsinki. His famous stackable wooden "Domus" chair was designed as part of this project.

Two mahogany side cabinets by Ole Wanscher, c.1955 with different brass handles and four tambour shutters. 51in (130cm) wide, **Q**

A dark stained and veneered birch Laukaan Pulu "Pirkka" sideboard, designed by Ilmari Tapiovaara c.1950. 47in (120cm) long, **Q**

A c.1960 chrome-plated steel and wicker armchair, model no.SZ01, by Martin Visser for Spectrum, with paper label. 27in (69cm), **L**

A 1960s black lacquered Asko "Mademoiselle" chair, designed by Ilmari Tapiovaara in 1958. 35in (89cm) high. **J**

Rare rosewood and steel "Stock" armchair, designed by Jens H. Quistgaard for Nissen c.1965, put together without bolts and can be completely disassembled. 27.5in (72cm) high, **N**

A c.1960s green lacquered lounge chair by Bjørn Winblad, with tufted pink cushion. 37in (94cm), **N**

A 1954 laminated wood "Casanova" armchair with red upholstery, designed by Ilmari Tapiovaara for Asko Oy, 40in (100cm) high, **L**

Italy

Just as the other war-ravaged countries of Europe found their way back from the brink of economic ruin, Italy emerged with prospects for recovery during the late 1940s. Its pre-war design strengths grew in maturity and by the 1950s, a new vigour had propelled Italy to be one of the most dynamic design centres in the world. Luminaries of pre-war innovation such as Gio Ponti (1891–1979) took up the challenge to reconstruct the country.

Italy's reputation for high standards of craftsmanship was well established: the automotive industry was highly innovative and the country's glass and ceramics were world-renowned – Ponti had even been the art director of ceramics manufacturer Richard Ginori from 1923 to 1930. However, functional, mass-produced construction systems and domestic items became symbolic of Italy's post-war renaissance. Designers such as Marco Zanuso (1916–2001) and the brothers Achille (1918–2002) and Pier Giacomo Castiglioni (1913–68) pushed the boundaries of industrial design, making it an acceptable form of consumerism. Modernity and comfort boosted the free-market appeal of everything from washing machines to furniture, lighting to decorative objects. This was a win-win situation for producers and consumers, with the new raft of young "rationalist" designers such as Franco Albini (1905–77), Vico Magistretti (1920–2006), and Ettore Sottsass (1917–2007)able to freely rebel against the fascist dictates of the previous era. His dynamic, sensual designs set architect Carlo Mollino (1905–73) apart among this band of visionary Italians. His glass-topped "Reale" table, made in 1949, sold at auction for a staggering $3.8 million dollars in 2005.

Just as American furniture manufacturer Knoll had nurtured its future talent, the Italian company Cassina, founded in 1927, weathered this tumultuous era by focusing on ground-breaking collaborations with designers such as Ponti and Albini. It was their vision that brought the best of Italian design and style to the consumer. This was the beginning of Italian predominance in the field of "ordinary things" – everyday functional objects with a good name attached, which attracted consumers in droves. It's a market that Italian companies and designers still triumph in today, as shown by the modern-day success of Alessi, founded in 1921. From post-war rationalism to the Pop-art aesthetics of Joe Colombo (1930–71) and Gaetano Pesce (b. 1939), Italian designers displayed a wonderful sense of playfulness and made Italy a worldwide leader in the field.

Left: A Piero Fornasetti single-drawer red metal file cabinet, printed with gold sunburst motif. 19.75in (50cm) wide, **M**

Below: A Gio Ponti sideboard of exceptional quality, the top portion with cabinet door and open shelves, the bottom with four doors concealing drawers and compartments fitted for shelves, drawers marked "Made in Italy". 78.75in (200cm) wide, **V**

Piero Fornasetti

(1913–88)

Born in Milan in 1913, Piero Fornasetti was a consummate magician. Few other 20th-century designers could have evolved such an idiosyncratic style, based as it was on the constant reinvention of historical references and motifs, while still producing a valid yet playful decorative antidote to the pared-down seriousness of many of their contemporaries.

Fornasetti, who was expelled from Milan's Brera Academy of Art in 1932, was idealistic and determined. His interrupted early training as a painter gave only a small hint of the amazing versatility to come; a versatility that was doubtless partly fuelled by the rebelliousness that later manifested in his approach to design. In the 1930s Fornasetti fell in love with the Surrealist movement, an obvious influence on much of his later work. The internationally famous architect and designer Gio Ponti championed Fornasetti early in his career – a friendship and collaboration that resulted in some of the most iconic designs of the 20th century, exemplified by the "Architettura" bureau-bookcase that they designed together in 1951.

Fornasetti's language is not difficult to decipher. His work is both traditional and witty; masterfully conceived with a playful juxtaposition that sets him apart from other artists and designers. Some argue that Fornasetti does little more than decorate surfaces, which in many respects is true, but no one else does it with such panache. Ponti said that Fornasetti "makes objects speak", and it's the skilful use of illusion, architectural perspectives, and adopted motifs that make him such an expert at "covering" other people's objects.

While Fornasetti's Surrealist influences are obvious, when combined with his fervent imagination his knowledge of historical styles and periods such as Mannerism, Neo-classicism, and the Renaissance enabled him to reproduce and reinvent an endless array of often humorous and instantly appealing designs. Signature leitmotifs already locked in the viewer's psyche, wittily transposed into something both thoroughly modern but appealingly traditional – perhaps this is where Fornasetti's unique skill lies.

Good

A limited edition plywood "Lyre" chair, designed in 1951. The seat is made of formed plywood, varnished, and silk-screen printed. The appeal of this piece lies in the juxtaposition of the chair's simplicity with the surreal nature of the decoration. This is simpler than many of Fornasetti's designs. 37in (94cm), **M**

Better

A two-door "Pompeian" corner cabinet, printed with an architectural façade with unique colouration in greys and black. This design is typical of Fornasetti's idea of giving a three-dimensional quality to something with a two-dimensional plane. This is a conversation piece – a real show stopper. 47in (199.5cm) wide, **Q**

Playing cards, fish, the sun and the moon – all these feature heavily in Fornasetti's eclectic decorative language. It was a language that he universally applied to almost every conceivable form: ceramics, furniture, ocean liners, interiors, fashion, bicycles, lamps, wastepaper bins – more than 11,000 items in total. One of Fornasetti's most recognizable and frequently recurring designs is his surreal reworking of the face of Lina Cavalieri, a 19th-century opera singer. Forming part of the "*Tema e Varazioni*" ("theme and variations") series, it was produced in more than 500 different versions and is still in production today. Fornasetti is a giant of Post-Modernist design, and his son Barnaba manages his legacy with strictly controlled issues of his highly sought-after designs.

Gio Ponti

Two "Superlegerra" chairs, designed by Gio Ponti for Cassina in 1957, lacquered ash, cellophane rush seats. 32.5in (83cm) high. **F**

Gio Ponti (1891-1979) is often cited as the father of modern Italian design. An accomplished architect, writer, and designer of ceramics and glass, he also produced a wide range of furniture designs, enjoying a prolific collaboration with Piero Fornasetti in the 1950s. He is perhaps best-known for his "Superleggera" chair, designed in 1957. Ponti's interpretation of the simple rustic chair is that rare thing, a design that seems at once ancient and utterly contemporary. It was hailed at the time as the lightest chair in the world, and has since become an icon of the era

Best

A four-panel screen decorated with hot air balloons, on casters. It is the size and unusual decoration of this piece that make it rare and particularly desirable. This piece makes a real statement. Each panel 79in (200cm) x 19.75in (50cm), **U**

A c.1950 four-drawer walnut dresser designed by Gio Ponti for M. Singer & Sons. 47in (119cm) wide, **U**

Furniture and lighting **57**

Joe Colombo

(1930–71)

Cesare "Joe" Colombo's star burned brightly, but sadly his life and career were cut short. Yet Colombo left the world of design and innovation a valuable legacy. He was obsessed by the future; even in the earliest years of his career, Colombo was driven by a vision of things to come, and he flourished in a period marked by advances in materials and production technology with the Space Race and Pop art and culture providing the impetus for his latent genius.

Colombo studied painting at the Brera Academy of Art in Milan, and it was there that he joined the avant-garde *Movimento Nucleare* art movement in 1951. He went on to study architecture at Milan's Polytechnic Institute, but when his father became ill in 1958, it fell to Joe and his brother Gianni to take on the family business: a factory producing electrical conductors. This industrial background allowed Colombo to experiment with a range of materials such as PVC, ABS, and polyethylene, leading to classics such as the "Universale No. 4860" stacking chair (1965–7) and the famous "Boby" storage trolley, designed in 1968 and still popular today.

Colombo created his own unique role in the world of design. The self-assembly "Tube" chair (1969–70), consisting of nesting tubular elements that can be configured in a variety of ways, is a playful spatial and marketing triumph. Colombo predicted changes in the traditional family, their future environment, and their increased mobility. Believing that people would require a "new type of habitat", he pursued a role as a "creator of the environment of the future". The "Total Furnishing Unit" (1971–72) epitomized these ideals and stands testament to one of the most forward-thinking designers of the 20th century.

Right: An "Elda" chair in bright yellow fibreglass with red wool upholstery, designed by Joe Colombo in 1963. With Stendig label. 37.25in (94cm) high, **L**

Below: A vinyl-covered "Tube" chair, designed by Joe Colombo, 1969–70, and manufactured by Flexform. The foam-covered cylindrical components can be arranged in a variety of ways, and also fit inside each other. 19.75in (49cm) diameter, nested, **P**

Italy

Italy was at the forefront of a post-war optimism in design. Advances in material technology and an insufficient supply of traditional materials such as wood opened the minds of forward-thinking designers, who by necessity had to explore new directions, using unusual combinations of materials to produce simple, functional, quality products.

The excitement of Italian design of this period lay in its diversity. An architect and designer, Osvaldo Borsani (1911–85) produced a large body of work in the 1940s and early 1950s, including case goods, storage pieces, and seating. In 1953, Osvaldo and his brother Fulgencio founded a firm called Tecno which, as its name suggests, became known for its research-and-technology-based approach to furniture design. Another notable architect and designer of the time was Carlo Mollino (1905–73), who once said that "Everything is permissible as long as it is fantastic."

Achille Castiglione (1918–2002) was an industrial designer renowned for frequently being inspired by everyday objects and ordinary materials. He set out to create forms with maximum effect while using the minimum amount of materials.

An Osvaldo Borsani/Tecno "L77" single adjustable bed on iron frame with red fabric upholstery, with Tecno labels. 76in (193cm) long, **P**

A 1970 "Fiocco" armchair, designed by Gruppo 14 for Busnelli. 43in (109cm) high, **M**

A 1957 "Mezzadoro" stool with chromium-plated steel stem and steam-treated beech foot-rest by Achille and Pier Giacomo Castiglioni. 20in (51cm) high, **L**

A c.1956 rosewood dining table by Osvaldo Borsani, with sculpted pedestal base and bronze sabots. 71in (180.5cm) wide, **O**

A 1940 "Leonardo" working table by Achille Castiglioni, with height-adjustable beech trestles and top coated with white plastic laminate. 78.75in (200cm) wide

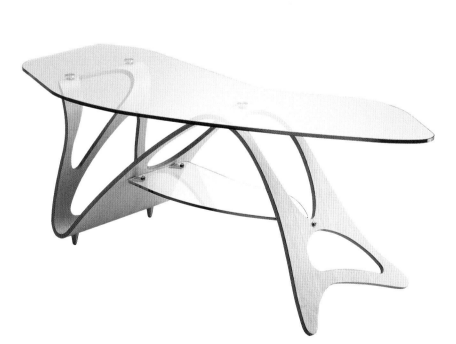

An "Arabesco" coffee table designed by Carlo Mollino in 1949, the plywood frame veneered with varnished beech. 50.75in (129cm) wide

A 1954 "Gilda" armchair by Carlo Mollino, with an ash frame and leather upholstery. The seat is adjustable. 27.5–36.5in (70–93cm) high

Italy

Post-war Italian furniture design was characterized by the use of a wide variety of materials. Marco Zanuso (1916–2001) was one of a group of Milanese designers who helped raise Italian furniture's international profile. One of Zanuso's key collaborations was with Arflex, a new division of Pirelli, for whom he designed seating with foam rubber upholstery. His "Antropus" chair was launched in 1949, while his "Lady" chair won first prize in the 1951 Milan Triennale.

Another important Milanese designer was Paolo Lomazzi (b. 1936), who founded a practice with Gionatan de Pas and Donato d'Urbino in 1966. The trio became famous in 1967 for "Blow", an inflatable armchair made of PVC film they designed for Zanotta. In 1968 they designed "Joe" for Poltronova, an armchair intended as a tribute to the American baseball player Joe DiMaggio. Their irreverent designs have become Pop culture icons.

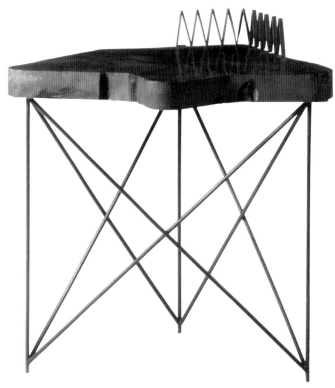

A 1950s walnut and painted iron corner table by Giovanni Ferrabini, on a triple X-form base. The top is formed as a single slab of walnut. 30in (76cm) high, **R**

A metal and upholstery "Lady" chair designed by Marco Zanuso for Arflex in 1951, unmarked. 33in (84cm) high, **L**

A carved maple and brass "Millepiedi" table, designed in 1953 by Franco Campo and Carlo Graffi manufactured in the 1980s, unmarked. Glass tabletop 84in (213cm) long, **Z**

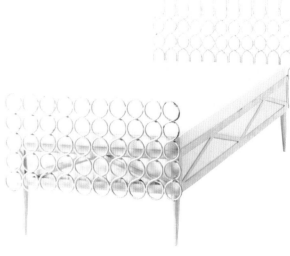

A 1969 "915" armchair with ottoman designed by
Carlo de Carli for Cinova, chrome-plated tubular
steel frame with leather upholstery. Chair 32.5in
(81cm) high, **L**

A 1950s white painted wrought
iron bed by Giovanni Ferrabini, the
impressive headboard formed as a
stylized coronet. 78.75in (200cm)
long, **U**

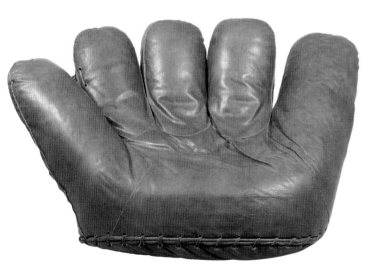

A leather-covered "Joe" armchair inamed after
the baseball legend Joe DiMaggio, designed by
Lomazzi/D'Urbino/De Pas for Poltronova in 1968.
37.5in (95cm) high, **N**

A c.1955 Alberto Marconetti armchair, its skeletal
oak frame reinforced by iron braces. The backrest
consists of woven leather straps. 40in (102cm)
high, **L**

North America

Considered one of the founding fathers of American Modernism, George Nelson (1908–86) trained as an architect at Yale before turning to product and interior design. His long association with office furniture and equipment manufacturer Herman Miller, where he was design director from 1945 to 1972, and the success of his own company George Nelson & Associates, which he founded in 1955, cemented his position as one of America's most important designers. Under his direction, these two companies produced many of the 20th century's most iconic pieces of furniture, in collaboration with American luminaries such as Charles (1907–78) and Ray Eames (1912–88), Harry Bertoia (1915–78), and Isamu Noguchi (1904–88). Nelson was also a prolific writer, and his pre-war meetings with – and subsequent articles on – several members of Europe's design elite, such as Gio Ponti (1891–1979), Le Corbusier (1887–1965), and Mies van der Rohe (1886–1969), helped introduce America to these "Modernist pioneers".

The concept of Mid-Century Modern as a design movement was readily embraced in the United States. Fuelled in part by pent-up consumer demand, affordable mortgages for the returning soldiers, and a baby boom, the country's post-war recovery was fast. Unlike its European allies, America hadn't suffered the devastation of its major cities or the subsequent shortages of materials being diverted to the rebuilding effort. Country dwellers flocked to the cities and demand for everything from cars to furniture spiralled. The new, more organic forms of Mid-Century Modernism were a refreshing progression of the more rigid International Style, and they worked well in the interiors of the light and airy American suburbs of the era, a style often referred to as "California Modern".

The large American design companies such as Knoll, Herman Miller, and George Nelson courted the best of the European designers: in fact, the pre- and post-war migration of many influential Europeans made for an extremely cosmopolitan roster. The son of Finnish architect Eliel Saarinen, Eero Saarinen (1910–61), had moved to the United States with his parents in 1923. His close working relationship with Charles and Ray Eames highlights the Scandinavian influence on the Mid-Century Modern movement, and Saarinen's designs for Knoll typify the sculptural, comfortable, and organic forms of this era: his "Grasshopper" chair (1946–7), "Womb" chair (1947–8), and "Tulip" chair (1955–6) are design classics.

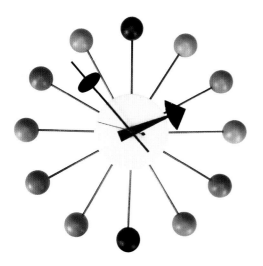

Left: A "Ball Clock" designed by George Nelson for Howard Miller in 1948, with enamelled metal hands and multi-coloured wooden spheres radiating from brass spokes. 13.25in (34cm) diam, **J**

Centre: An early Florence Knoll/ Knoll credenza on an ebonized base, with sea grass-lined sliding doors, unmarked. 72in (183cm) wide, **T**

Below: A Vladimir Kagan "Floating Curve" sofa with a sculptural walnut frame, upholstered in indigo chenille. 82.5in (209.5cm) wide, **U**

Charles and Ray Eames

(1907–78 and 1912-88)

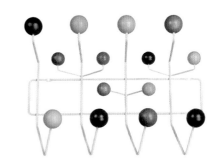

Charles and Ray Eames make up one of the 20th-century's most enduring design partnerships. They were married in 1941, and their eclectic "West Coast" combination of interests and imagination fostered a joint career that spanned more than forty years and resulted in some of the most innovative and influential furniture designs of the post-war period.

The couple's big, mass-production break came in the form of a moulded plywood leg-splint which the US Navy ordered by the thousands. This experimentation with materials and manufacturing techniques was to become a trademark of their progressive talents. Early products such as the "LCW" (short for "lounge chair wood") chair of 1945 offer a mere hint of the great things that were to come in a variey of disciplines, from architecture to film. Built in Los Angeles in 1949, the Eames House (also known as Case Study House No. 8) is an influential experiment in low-cost housing. The Eameses were not afraid of clutter and filled their home with inspirational objects covering every facet of design. In their time they collaborated with giants such as Hermann Miller and IBM.

The post-war period of American prosperity, which created an increasingly affluent and design-conscious society, provided the perfect platform for their innovative use of materials. Launched by Herman Miller in 1956, their moulded plywood and leather lounge chair with its matching ottoman represent the essence of this great partnership.

Top: An Eames "Hang-It-All" coat rack, designed in 1953, with 14 coloured wood balls on an enameled metal frame. Produced by Herman Miller, this example is of recent manufacture. 19.5in (50cm) wide, **C**

Below left: A pair of Eames "Armshell" 1945 chairs, dowel-leg fibreglass with moulded marks and paper labels. The wood bases are later production. 31in (77.5cm) high, **L**

Below right: A 1945–6 Eames moulded plywood "LCW" chair, produced by Evans Products and distributed by Herman Miller. 26.75in (68cm) high, **M**

Opposite: A 1955 Eames "ESU" wall unit, with zinc-coated steel supports, plywood shelves, and wire rod cross supports on sides and back.. 65in (165cm) high, **R**

North America

After working for Raymond Loewy, I. M. Pei, and Eero Saarinen, architect and designer Warren Platner (1919–2006) opened his own office in 1967. The "Platner Collection", a series of chairs, ottomans, and tables he developed for Knoll in the 1960s, forms his major contribution to mid-century furniture design. Platner designed both the structure and the production method – the sculptural bases were made of hundreds of rods and some chairs required more than a thousand welds.

Best known for the moulded plywood seating line he created for Plycraft, Norman Cherner (1920–87) also wrote about his theories in books such as *Make Your Own Modern Furniture* (1953) and *How to Build a House for Less than $6,000* (1960).

Two design luminaries from this period are Vladimir Kagan (b. 1927) and Eero Saarinen (1910–61), who had emigrated to the United States from Germany and Finland respectively. Kagan's sculptural, organic furniture forms with trademark splayed legs and sinuous frames look like direct descendants of Finn Juhl's chairs, while Saarinen's work represented the fusion of Scandinavian Modernism with an American corporate aesthetic.

A 1957 "Cherner" armchair designed by Norman Cherner for Plycraft, constructed from bent laminated wood with a nut-wood veneer. 26.5in (67cm) wide, **L**

A glass-topped coffee table with steel wire rod base in a bronze finish, designed by Warren Platner in 1966 for Knoll. Base 30in (76cm), **K**

A c.1955 John Risley wire chair, in the form of a woman, and circular ottoman. 40in (102cm) high, **M**

An unusual Vladimir Kagan drop-leaf, gateleg
dining table on seven-legged wood base.
Unmarked. 66.5in (169cm) long (fully extended), **N**

A "Grasshopper" chair, designed by Eero Saarinen
for Knoll in 1946, with corduroy upholstery. 34.5in
(87.5cm) high, **M**

A 1950 Vladimir Kagan "Serpentine" sofa
upholstered in red fabric. 92in (233.5cm) wide, **T**

North America

While modernist design quickly became the status quo in the United States, a number of designers pursued an aesthetic closer to the Arts and Crafts movement. Many of them worked at perfecting their handicraft at a time when craftsmanship was considered a relic of the past. The pioneer of this approach was Wharton Esherick (1887–1970), known as the "Dean of American Craftsmen". Phillip Lloyd Powell (1919-2008) was another exponent of studio furniture. His work incorporates diverse materials, from metal and wood to slate and marble, chosen for their tactile qualities.

Although never formally trained as a designer, Paul McCobb (1917–69), set up his own successful industrial design company, Paul McCobb Design Associates, in New York. In 1950, he launched the "Planner Group", a line of affordable, modular home furnishings with clean, modern lines. Perfectly suited to post-war middle-class lifestyles, the line was an immediate success.

A Phillip Lloyd Powell walnut bench, with woven ecru fabric cushions and integrated marble top table. 100.5in (255cm) wide, **V**

A Paul McCobb three-drawer maple dresser, with brass pulls. 36in (91cm) wide, **L**

An Edward Wormley / Dunbar, walnut chest with six drawers and circular brass pulls. 38in (97cm) wide, **M**

George Nakashima

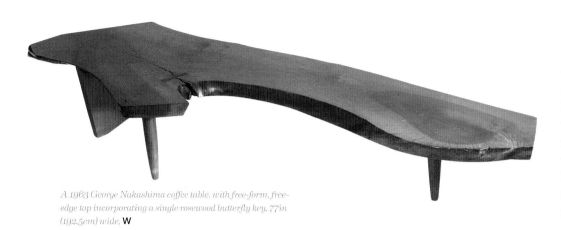

A 1963 George Nakashima coffee table, with free-form, free-edge top incorporating a single rosewood butterfly key. 77in (192.5cm) wide, **W**

Trained as an architect, George Nakashima (1905–90) worked in Paris, Tokyo, and an Indian ashram before returning to Seattle in 1940 to open a furniture workshop. As a Japanese American, he was held in an internment camp after the attack on Pearl Harbor. After his release, he settled in New Hope, Pennsylvania, and devoted himself to working in wood. His designs rely entirely on the inherent qualities of the material; he selected the wood carefully, preferring pieces with outstanding burls, good colour and natural "uro" or recessed areas. Many of his pieces have an unworked free edge to express the natural form of the wood

A Wharton Esherick walnut Captain's chair, with woven leather seat. 30.25in (77cm) high, **S**

A walnut modular wall unit by Paul McCobb, from the "Connoisseur" collection for H. Sacks & Sons, with 'McCobb' metal tag. 147.5in (374.5cm) wide, **N**

Knoll International

Below left: The 1954 "Lounge Chair no.31" was designed by Florence Knoll for Knoll International, chromium plated tubular steel with foam upholstery. 29.5in (75cm) high, **L**

Below right: A deep-buttoned black leather chair, raised on square chrome legs, designed by Florence Knoll. **D**

Opposite: A "Parallel Bar System" lounge chair designed by Florence Knoll for Knoll in 1955. 30in (76cm) high, **L**

Hans Knoll was a man with vision. The son of a prominent German furniture designer, he was born in Stuttgart in 1914. In 1937, he emigrated to New York and established his own furniture company, Knoll, the following year. Thanks to his cosmopolitan education and upbringing, Hans had already established a good network of connections in the contemporary design world. His vision was simple but revolutionary for the time: he realized that architects would need well-designed furniture with which to fill their modern buildings.

Hans Knoll hired a well-qualified young woman called Florence Schust. As well as holding degrees in architecture and design, she had worked and studied with luminaries such as Mies van der Rohe, Marcel Breuer, and Walter Gropius. Hans married her in 1946, and together they formed Knoll Associates. Florence gave the company creative impetus, focusing on superlative design quality and efficient, innovative production techniques. The idea of paying designers a royalty and crediting their work was ground-breaking and helped to attract established designers; at the same time, the couple also realized that it was of paramount importance to nurture up-and-coming talent. Eero Saarinen and Franco Albini were soon working with people such as Harry Bertoia and Isamu Noguchi. By also acquiring the rights to produce the already iconic designs of Mies van der Rohe and Marcel Breuer, the company was establishing itself as an international force.

By 1947 Knoll had opened a textiles showroom, mainly in response to the shortage of suitable fabrics for its products, and the collections were an immediate success. The purchase of a factory in Pennsburg, Pennsylvania, was soon followed by the opening of another in nearby East Greenville, which remains Knoll's headquarters and manufacturing base. Knoll essentially invented the idea of corporate interior design, and its Planning Unit was the model for many later companies.

When Hans Knoll was killed in a car crash in 1955, it fell to Florence to assume the presidency of the company. She retired in 1965, but her words are still synonymous with the company's ideals: "Good design is good business." Knoll's commitment to the integrity and quality of good design has cemented its position as an international leader in the field – it's little wonder that the company's roster of designers reads like a directory of the world's greatest design talent.

Knoll
International

Top: Florence Knoll referred to her 1961 line of desks, which included this rosewood partner's desk, as the "meat and potatoes" needed to fill the gaps in the Knoll collection. 72in (183cm wide), **N**

Centre: The spare, angular design of this black laquered iron and white-laminate extension table, designed by Florence Knoll c.1965, is a striking example of the Mid-Century Modern aesthetic. 27.5in (70cm) high, **J**

Below right: A pair of Florence Knoll for Knoll dressers, each with woodgrain laminate top and three louvre-front drawers, on tubular black metal legs, normal wear, unmarked. 36in (91.5cm) high, **L**

Opposite, top: Florence Knoll's 1954 "Lounge" collection has secured its place in the pantheon of modern classics. The series includes a lounge chair, benches, and the two-seater sofa shown here. 31.25in (78cm) high, **O**

Opposite, bottom: Florence Knoll / Knoll, walnut credenza with four-doors concealing fitted drawers and adjustable shelves, on chromed steel legs. 71.5in (182cm) wide, **K**

Wendell Castle

(b. 1932)

Top: A painted wood side table, original prototype designed and manufactured by Wendell Castle, c.1969.

Bottom, left: A 1973 laminated wood pedestal by Wendell Castle, signed "W.C. 73". 20in (51cm) high, **U**

Bottom right: A "Molar Group" swivel coffee table in black gel-coated fiberglass-reinforced plastic, designed and manufactured by Wendell Castle c.1969.

Opposite: A 1963 Wendell Castle sculpted oak sleigh chair, with hard leather sling seat, signed "WE 63". 34.5in (87.5cm) high, **EE**

Wendell Castle is a name that strikes fear into some and calls forth admiration in others, perhaps in part because it is almost impossible to define the work of this talented, often whimsical man. Born in 1932, Castle studied both fine art and industrial design at the University of Kansas, a combination of disciplines that helps blur the often all too rigid boundaries between the different categories of people working in the design world.

Preferring to be called a "furniture artist" rather than a designer, Wendell has continually challenged perceptions, creating sculptural and organic pieces in a variety of materials such as plastics, bronze, steel, and wood. Made of glass-reinforced polyester and undeniably tooth-like in appearance, his "Molar" chairs and coffee tables of the 1960s are Pop classics but regarded with less reverence than the work of some of his European counterparts.

It's plain to see that Castle is a craftsman and a sculptor, unafraid of taking risks and producing theatrical, highly individual works that cock a snook at function in reverence to the skill of the artisan. Castle has often been accused of "forsaking function in favour of form". In reality, there are no real rules about the conformity between form and function and if Castle chooses to ignore or camouflage it on occasion, then it is his right as an artist to do so.

Castle's use of sculptural biomorphic forms are central to his identity but his playfulness and often misunderstood irony are what set him apart from many other post-war and contemporary designers. Always innovative and experimental in his use of materials, Castle continues to question the boundaries between art, design, and industrial application. These pieces can be both challenging and massively rewarding, but it is this inspirational creativity that put him at the forefront of post-war American design. Castle is generally considered the most important furniture artist of the era.

George Nelson

(1908–86)

Industrial designer, writer, and architect George Nelson (1908–86) is regarded as one of the founders of American Modernism. While Director of Design at the Herman Miller furniture company, Nelson introduced the designs of such luminaries as Harry Bertoia (1915-78) and Isamu Noguchi (1904-88).

Tommi Parzinger (1903–81) studied design at the School of Art and Craft in his native Munich before moving to New York in 1932. He was closer in approach to an 18th-century French *ébéniste* or cabinetmaker than an industrial designer – his work is best described as "High-Style Modernism". Most of the luxurious pieces he created involved craft-intensive materials and processes, such as coloured lacquer and hand-crafted brasswork.

Harvey Probber (1922–2003) started selling his designs to New York funiture manufacturers when he was still at high school. He set up his own furniture company in 1945, and went on to introduce flexible modular seating units that could be grouped in a variety of ways.

A c.1969 Harvey Probber upholstered bent mirror aluminium armchair, with paper label and copy of original buyer's receipt. 27.5in (70cm) wide, **M**

A c.1960 "Marshmallow" sofa, designed by Iriving Harper (often credited to George Nelson) for Herman Miller, 18 leather-covered cushions on a lacquered tubular steel frame. 50in (130cm) long, **Q**

A Tommi Parzinger bleached mahogany sideboard, with three central drawers, and brass fittings. 65.5in (166.5cm) wide, **R**

An enamelled metal and wooden "Spike" wall clock, designed c.1952 by George Nelson for Howard Miller, with "Howard Miller Clock Company" decal. 18in (46cm) diam, **E**

A Harvey Probber mahogany and brass credenza with caned doors; unmarked. 62.75in (159cm) wide, **L**

A George Nelson laminate, metal and wood cabinet for Herman Miller, single yellow drawer over two sliding doors raised on black metal frame, label in drawer. 33.5in (85cm) wide, **K**

Lighting

Architects and designers have always diversified – from door handles to lighting, the post-war demand for home furnishings ensured the liveliest minds were producing designs that would unify rooms. Mid-Century Modern lighting has a futuristic, pared-down feel, making the most of new fabrication techniques, while plastics played an important part in new forms of sculptural lighting. The Italians were world leaders in this field. Founded in 1946, Arredoluce embodied innovative style, working with designers such as Gino Sarfatti (1912–85). Flos, home of the designs of the Castiglioni brothers, was another influential manufacturer.

French sculptor Serge Mouille (1922–88) advocated a simpler style, making his lamps by hand. His aluminium shades allow light to be dispersed over a wide area. He worked to achieve a kinetic, sculptural aesthetic that evoked a sense of movement in space. Danish manufacturer Louis Poulsen collaborated with visionary designers to produce iconic lighting solutions; Poul Henningsen's "Artichoke" hanging lamp (1958) is now considered a timeless classic.

An Arredoluce "Triennale" three-arm floor lamp, c.1950 (no. 12128), designed by Gino Sarfatti, with enameled metal shades. Post 66in (168cm) high, **P**

A "Lampadaire" floor lamp designed by Serge Mouille c.1950. Aluminium shade with black exterior and white reflective interior with adjustable ball-joint and black lacquered base. 65in (165 cm) high, **P**

A Tommi Parzinger floor lamp with eight tall candlestick fixtures on black iron base. 72in (180cm) high, **N**

An iconic "Arco" lamp, designed by Achille and Pier Castiglioni for Flos in 1962. The curved stainless steel arm ends in a tulip shade, supported on a rectangular marble base. 96in (244cm) high, **L**

A 1960s futuristic chromed metal "satellite" table lamp, with six arms, each terminating in a spherical shade with a single socket, arms rotate on a baluster-form base. 26.75in (68cm) high, **L**

A T.H. Robsjohn-Gibbings brass table lamp for Hansen with ecru paper shade, white enamelled metal reflector, and three sockets. Corseted brass tripod base, reflector stamped "Hansen/New York". 21.5in (55cm) high, **M**

A copper and steel "Artichoke" lamp desgined by Poul Hennigsen for Louis Poulsen, in 1957. 18in (46cm) high, **N**

A pair of Arredoluce chrome, cylindrical lamps, with red enamelled balls. 9.5in (24cm) high, **L**

A 1960s Valenti Pistillo ceiling light, of clustered ball and arm, or anenome, design. 25in (64cm) diameter, **C**

A late 1960s Ingo Maurer/M Design injection-moulded lamp, in the form of a 60-watt light bulb 24in (60cm) high, **H**

Germany
and Central Europe

Modernism symbolizes for many a rejection of traditional forms and an acceptance of a new social, economic, and industrial-based future. The evolution of European Mid-Century Modernism borrows strongly from this purity but would be incomplete without the influence of other ideologies.

In central Europe, some designers, such as Kurt Thut (1931–2011) and (Egon Eiermann (1904–70), who was one of Germany's leading architects of the time, stuck to their Functionalist roots. Others, however, delighted in the possibilities afforded by new materials. Günter Beltzig (b. 1941), who started his career designing electrical goods for Siemens, became known in the 1960s for his innovative plastic furniture, produced by the manufacturing company he had set up with his brothers. In 1968 Beltzig designed the plastic "Floris" chair, which was inspired by the imminent moon landing.

A 1970s Horn "Kangaroo" armchair, designed by Ernst Moeckl. The chair is moulded from "Baydur". 30.5in (76.5cm) high, **C**

A wooden construction sideboard with blue-grey pavatex glass sliding doors and chrome-plated tubular steel legs. Designed in 1953 by Kurt Thut, manufacured by Teo Jakob 45in (113cm) high **M**

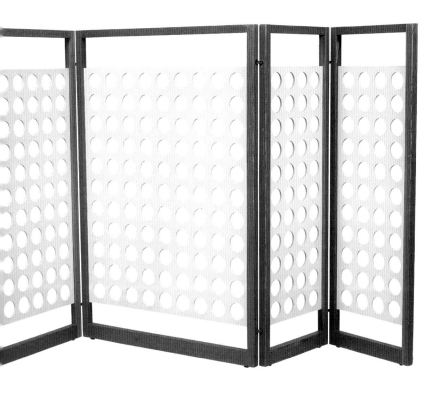

Screen designed by Egon Eiermann in 1968 for the House of Represenatives of the German Bundestag in Bonn. 56 in (142cm) high, **Q**

An "E10" woven rattan lounge chair designed by Egon Eiermann c.1949, manufactured by H. Murmann, 32in (81cm)high, **I**

An anthropomorphic "Floris" chair in fibreglass, designed by Günter Beltzig in 1967, manufactured by Gebrüder Beltzig, 42in (107cm) high, **L**

A 1968 fibreglass "Garden Egg" chair with upholstered interior and articulated top, designed by Peter Ghyczy for Reuter Products. 39.5 in (100cm) high open, **J**

A pair of 1966 "Galaxy" armchairs designed by Walter Pichler for R. Svoboda & Co, in glazed, naturally anodized aluminum plate. 27.5 in (70cm) high

France

If making sense of innumerable different design movements is difficult, defining or categorizing the work of individual designers can be equally daunting. Jacques Adnet (1901–84), was the master of French Art Deco Modernism. He took part in the famous Paris Exhibition of 1925 (officially known as the *Exposition Internationale des Arts Décoratifs et Industriels Modernes*) at which the term "Art Deco" was coined. Even as a young man, Adnet was distinctly avant-garde; his pared-down approach was nevertheless both stylish and luxurious. His clever juxtaposition of materials such as glass, metal, exotic woods, leather, fish skin, and parchment set the benchmark for much to come. Adnet's role as director of La Compagnie des Arts Français from 1928 to 1960, where he worked with designers such as Charlotte Perriand (1903–99), ensured his position as an important post-war designer. He was involved in many major projects such as presidential commissions and, in 1950, the design of the armchairs for the UNESCO conference rooms in Paris.

In the aftermath of World War II, Adnet's luxurious, modern approach offered no solution to the immediate needs of a war-torn country with massive housing shortages. The flattened city of Le Havre became a prototype for collective living: reinforced concrete tower blocks of compact rooms with fitted interiors and mass-produced furniture, were to become the post-war reality for many French people. The stylish, simple furniture designed by René Gabriel (1890-1950) and Marcel Gascoin (1907–86) proved to be a way of filling the 20,000 apartments the government hoped to build every month.

As France gradually recovered its economic strength, a new generation of designers began to experiment with new materials and forms. The austerity of post-war design was replaced by a vigorous interest in more hedonistic styles. French society was becoming more subversive and rebellious; so too were their designs for life. Pierre Paulin (1927–2009) experimented with swimwear fabric, rubber, and foam to produce designs such as the "Ribbon" chair (1965) and "Tongue" chair (1967), both sculptural masterpieces. Similarly, the low-slung pieces Olivier Mourgue (b. 1939) designed for his "Djinn" series (1965) were highly suggestive of a more laid-back approach to life (in 1968, the "Djinn" chair was famously used in Stanley Kubrick's film *2001: A Space Odyssey*). Known in France as the *mobi-boom*, this was an explosive period for design that lasted from 1945 to the mid 1970s.

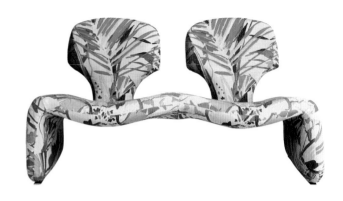

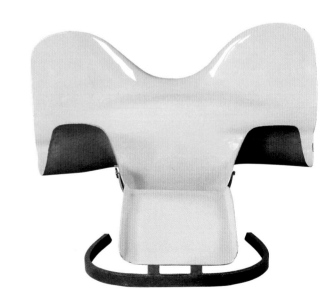

Le Corbusier

(1887–1965)

Charlotte Perriand

(1903–99)

Below: A 1953 "Bibliothèque" designed by Charlotte Perriand and Jean Prouvé, with enameled aluminium and pine shelving unit on pine long bench. From La Maison de la Tunisie at the Cité Universitaire, Paris. 138in (351cm) wide, **X**

Opposite, top: A 1960s metal-framed basculant chair, by Le Corbusier, Charlotte Perriand and Pierre Jeanneret, model no. B301, chromed bent tubular steel frame, calfskin seat and back with slung leather arms, probably manufactured by Cassina or Aram. 26.75in (68cm) wide, **K**

Opposite, bottom: A room partition (cabinet) with Formica sliding doors, designed by Le Corbusier in 1957, in oak with white lacquered plywood and green linoleum. This type of storage unit with sliding doors and trays that could be accessed from two sides was developed by Le Corbusier for the "Cité Radieuse" housing development in Firminy, and was also used in Rezé. 75in (188cm) long, **U**

Known as Le Corbusier, a pseudonym he adopted in his early thirties, Charles-Edouard Jeanneret is one of the giants of 20th-century architecture and design, and a founding father of the modernist movement. Born in Switzerland in 1887, he studied art and architecture in his early years and worked for renowned architects in France and Germany before setting up his own office in Paris after World War I (he became a French citizen in 1930). Le Corbusier's pioneering work in architecture addressed the political aspects of affordable housing and the aesthetics, form, and function of human needs. This was his "manifesto", as laid out in his collection of essays, *Vers une architecture* ("Toward an architecture"), published in 1923. The Villa Savoye on the outskirts of Paris, built between 1929 and 1931, is one of his greatest achievements – pure Le Corbusier.

In 1927, a young designer called Charlotte Perriand visited Le Corbusier's studio to ask if she could work for him. She was famously dismissed with the comment, "We don't embroider cushions here." This attitude summed up the chauvinism that was prevalent at the time. Born in 1903, Perriand had studied at the school attached to the Paris Museum of Applied Arts, but its emphasis on the Beaux-Arts style and crafts did not sit well with her radical ideas. Keen to experiment with the methods used to produce bicycles and automotive parts, she was fascinated with the "machine-age aesthetic".

Le Corbusier was soon forced to revise his earlier hasty judgment: his cousin and collaborator, Pierre Jeanneret, showed him the glass and steel rooftop bar Perriand had designed for the *Salon d'Automne* exhibition in Paris, and she joined his studio not long after. This was the start of one of the greatest design collaborations of the 20th century. There seems to be no record of Le Corbusier making furniture prior to meeting Perriand, and while their radical ideas were not particularly well received at first, their tubular metal constructions, such as the "LC2 Grand Confort" armchair and the "B306" *chaise-longue*, both designed in 1928, have become legendary style icons. Today, there are many copies of these timeless classics, but Cassina is the only company licensed by the Le Corbusier Foundation to produce these designs.

Le Corbusier's philosophy profoundly affected contemporary ideas on city planning and he worked with many other famous architects, but he has been heavily criticized in some circles for creating an unassailable myth. Perriand was forever in his shadow and not given due credit for her massive influence on design. It was her "spirit of enquiry" that motivated her, and Perriand's subsequent projects with notable designers and artists such as Jean Prouvé and Fernand Léger emphasize the integrity of both her collaborative and individual work, which is borne out by the enduring popularity of her designs.

Jean Prouvé

(1901–84)

Top: A "Visiteur" armchair, designed by Jean Prouvé in 1942 and manufactured c.1950 by Les Ateliers Jean Prouvé in Nancy. Red lacquered and bent tubular iron, laminated oak seat and backrest, solid oak armrests and ball feet. 29in (74cm) high, **W**

Bottom: A c.1955 Esconde sideboard, circle of Jean Prouvé, from a line of furniture produced for student housing in Paris. Natural and red lacquered beechwood veneer, black lacquered perforated sheet metal feet. 36in (92 cm) high, **M**

Opposite: An oak and painted steel student desk and chair unit by Jean Prouvé, with sliding iron inkwell. 32in (81cm) long, **M**

"Never design anything that cannot be made" – wise words from one of the greatest French designers of the 20th century. Born in 1901, Jean Prouvé was a skilled craftsman with an artistic family background. His father, the painter and sculptor Victor Prouvé, was already famous as a founder of the Nancy School. Jean's dream of becoming an engineer was interrupted by stints in the army and as an apprentice artisan blacksmith. However, by 1923 he had his own workshops in Nancy and quickly progressed from the bread-and-butter world of ornamental grilles to highly innovative metal pressing and welding. It was the potential of mass-production techniques in metal, and his commercial success with metal office furniture and designs such as the later iconic "Standard" chair (1934), that spurred him on to pursue the architectural side of mass production.

For many years, Prouvé's practical nature somehow denied him the label of designer; he categorized himself as "a factory man". During and immediately after the war, he focused largely on prefabricated buildings and wood furniture. It was only when he lost control of his company in 1953 that Prouvé flowered into the designer so revered in France and across the world today. Buildings such as the Evian Pump Room (1956–7) vindicate his vision of the evolution of industrial processes and spatial awareness. Without him, modern architects would not have the technical understanding of construction materials that they have today.

Switzerland

Design in post-war Switzerland evolved into an uncomplicated abstract style devoid of geographic or historical references, but wrought from pre-war elements of Futurism and Constructivism. Prominent Swiss designers such as architect Hans Bellman (1911–90) had trained at the Bauhaus in Dessau and Berlin, but returned to Switzerland before the war to work independently. Bellman, who had worked as an architect in the studio of Mies van der Rohe, was one of the forerunners of classical Modernism. Characterized by an absolute economy of means and clear, unornamented forms, his designs include the "Popsicle" tripod table from the 1950s, manufactured by Knoll.

Although Swiss-born architect Pierre Jeanneret (1896–1967) is overshadowed by his more famous cousin, Le Corbusier, he made a significant contribution to pre- and post-war design. It's largely due to his influence that the historic collaboration between Charlotte Perriand and Le Corbusier ever took place, and the three of them went on to produce some of the 20th century's defining designs. Jeanneret also designed large amounts of the civic architecture of the "new" northern Indian city of Chandigarh (of which Le Corbusier was a principal architect) as well as furniture used in the city's administrative buildings.

A "Sitwell" lounge chair, designed by Hans Bellmann for Strässle in 1958. With steel legs and fibreglass seat shell, upholstered in polyester foam and red fabric. 34in (87cm) high, **L**

A set of stacking stools, designed in 1960 by Michel Péclard (1911-1996) for Horgen Glarus, and manufactured in 1964. Ivory lacquered laminated wood, all parts with paper labels (partly illegible): Horgen Glarus Aifd. 18in (46cm) high, **L**

A c.1955 teak and leather desk, designed by
Pierre Jeanneret for the Chandigarh Administration
Building, India. 27.5in (71cm) high, **T**

A 1968 "Cubo" polyutherane couch,
designed by Johannes Larrson for
France & Son. 21.5in (54.5cm) wide, **H**

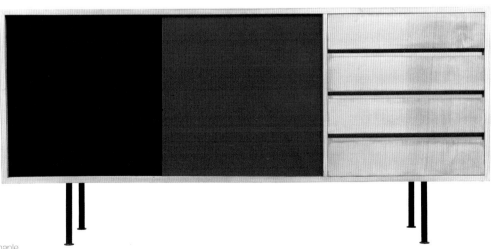

A c.1958–60 Wohnbedarf AG sideboard, in maple
veneer, with red and black glass sliding doors, and
black lacquered metal legs. 63in (160cm) long, **L**

Britain

Far from stifling design creativity, World War II was a rich period of innovation and ingenious application. Most of these innovations were for military purposes, but the post-war period saw designers, newly released from their military shackles, catapulted into a new world of optimistic opportunity. This was particularly apparent in Britain, where the post-war shortages of materials, especially wood, demanded a new way of thinking – a new direction.

In 1946, the Victoria and Albert Museum in London hosted the Britain Can Make It exhibition. Aimed at boosting morale, it allowed designers such as Ernest Race (1913–64) to present innovative work, such as the "BA3" dining chair made from cast-aluminium components. This technology had been pioneered for aircraft and vehicle manufacture, and designers adapted mass-production techniques and industrial materials to fit domestic and commercial interiors. Onerous as they must have seemed, the post-war austerity measures imposed by the government proved to be surprisingly inspirational to the designers of the period.

Left: A late 1960s Archie Shine Limited oval rosewood veneered dinning table, raised on aluminium legs united by a rosewood veneered stretcher. 78.75in (200cm) wide, **H**

Below: A c.1963 Isokon "Penguin Donkey Mark II" bookcase, designed by Ernest Race, with white-painted shelves on square supports. 21in (53cm) wide, **D**

As the economy improved and consumer demand and confidence increased, the public started to look for more exciting furniture, fabrics, and lighting. In 1951, the Festival of Britain, which was held to give the British people a "sense of recovery", provided a platform for myriad new designers and fresh ideas by showcasing advances in architecture, arts, science, design, and film. Attracting more than ten million visitors, the event has become enshrined in British history as an invaluable boost to the post-war nation. The whole premise of the festival was to advocate "good design", and it was here that Race's creations were utilized. His light, elegant "Antelope" chair graced the terraces of the newly built Royal Festival Hall in London, its thin steel-rod construction and ball feet redolent of atomic and molecular models.

Often compared to Charles and Ray Eames, Robin (1915–2010) and Lucienne Day (1917–2010) are Britain's most famous design duo. The "Hillestak" chair of 1950 bought low-cost modern design to the public. The Festival of Britain also proved to be a perfect stage for their work; Robin's innovative furniture solutions were used throughout the exhibition, and ranged from restaurant seating to orchestra chairs. It was a diverse and demanding brief, culminating in such classics as his armchair designed for the Royal Festival Hall. His furnishings were complemented by "Calyx", one of Lucienne's revolutionary fabric designs, and the couple's place in design history was cemented. Robin Day's "Polyprop" stacking chair (1962–3) remains the ultimate low-cost seating solution and is the best-selling chair of all time.

Mass production

Mass production is synonymous with low-cost goods made for a burgeoning consumer society after World War II, but the idea of bringing stylish housing, furniture, and other durables to the masses motivated many of the best designers of the 20th century.

The mainstay of many a home in the 1960s and 1970s, Ercol is the epitome of high-quality, modern British furniture. The company was founded in 1920 by Lucian Ercolani. Working with the latest steam-bending processes, he created simple chair and table designs. While Ercol furniture is often considered traditional, it shared many characteristics with successful Scandinavian designs. Many original designs are still in production and affordable today. In the UK, Ercol produces Ercol Originals, a range of 1950s designs that includes both the "Butterfly" chair and the "Love Seat" settee shown here. Other British firms of note are G Plan, Stag, and Merrow Associates.

Two steambent "Butterfly" chairs, designed by Lucian Ercolani for Ercol in 1958. 17in (43cm) wide, **D**

An Ercol elm double seat "Love Seat" settee, with spindle back. 44.25in (112.5cm) wide, **D**

A set of three elm Ercol "Pebble" nesting tables, 1956. Largest 25in (65cm) wide, **E**

A Merrow Associates chrome and rosewood
veneer occasional table, with glass top. 22.5in
(56cm) wide, **H**

A late 1960s–70s Merrow Associates rosewood
and chromed-steel desk, probably designed by
Richard Young. 48in (122cm) wide, **M**

A c.1970 G-Plan sideboard, with three drawers
above two hinged covers, raised on ebonised legs.
59in (150cm) wide, **D**

Brazil

Historically, Brazil's artistic identity had been heavily reliant on European and colonial influences. Many Brazilian artists and designers were trained in Europe and were constrained by "old-school" ideals. Brazil needed a more "home-grown" style and this move towards a true Brazilian identity began to take shape in the early 20th century, based on a re-evaluation of cultural influences and indigenous materials. Architecture and the arts eagerly drew from popular European influences such as Modernism, Cubism, and Surrealism, but reinterpreted them in a way that was relevant to Brazilian culture.

Many regard Joaquim Tenreiro (1906–92), as the founding father of Brazilian Modernist furniture design. He was at the heart of this Brazilian renaissance. Influenced by Le Corbusier, the distinct concrete Modernism of Brazilian buildings was already evolving. Where timber and steel were less abundant, concrete triumphed, while the local sunshine dictated the distinctive *brise-soleil* (sun-blind) facades of these spectacular new edifices. The inimitable style of architect Oscar Niemeyer (b. 1907) was in the ascendancy, and Tenreiro was soon supplying his projects with classics such as the "Poltrona Leve", a light armchair designed in 1942. Sculptural, well crafted, and suited to their environment, his designs utilized indigenous materials as well as meeting the requirements of the market; wicker and exotic hardwoods define his work.

Left: A "Sleepwalker's Arm Chair" in ivory wood, designed by Joaquim Tenreiro in 1950. 28in (71cm) high

Below: This lounge chair and ottoman were originally designed by Oscar and Ana Maria Niemeyer for the headquarters of the French Communist Party in Paris in 1972. Chair 69in (174cm) long, **U**

This collaboration of designers, architects, and artists is nothing new. Niemeyer's influence cannot be understated and the scale of his work provided many Brazilian designers with a sturdy platform. José Zanine Caldas (1918–2001), Sérgio Rodrigues (b. 1927), and Ricardo Fasanello (1930–93) have all at one time produced pieces designed to grace the Modernist buildings of Brazil's premier architect. True to the Brazilian tradition, the mid-century designs of all three men focus on the use of indigenous woods and materials. Traditional woodworking skills are combined with contemporary shapes, with no detriment to the natural products used. The reverence to these natural origins is exemplified in the work of Rodrigues, whose elegant "Cantu" chair (c.1959) and robust "Sheriff" chair (1957) are pure Brazil. The beautiful grain of jacaranda, rosewood, and peroba marks many of these South American classics so revered by modern collectors.

Sérgio Rodrigues

(b. 1927)

Right: Low-backed "Cantu" dining chairs, designed by Sérgio Rodrigues in 1967. 32in (81cm) high

Below: A 1960s rosewood bookshelf by Sérgio Rodrigues. 81in (205.5cm) long

Opposite, top left: A "Vronka" lounge chair with jacaranda frame and upholstered seat, designed by Sérgio Rodrigues in 1962. 35 in (89cm) high

Opposite, top right: A rare cabinet in jacaranda, designed by Sérgio Rodrigues for Oca Industries in the 1960s. 77in (195.5cm) long

Opposite, bottom: An ISA "Sheriff" sofa, designed by Sérgio Rodrigues in 1957, in tropical hardwood with black leather cushions, with "ISA" label. 81in (205cm) wide, **O**

Born in 1927 and a native of Rio de Janeiro, Sérgio Rodrigues is a major exponent of Brazilian Modernism. He trained as an architect, and his work found great favour in the post-war Utopian vision that was Brasilia, the principal designer of which was the great architect Oscar Niemeyer. This "brave new world", built from scratch under the direction of Niemeyer and Lúcio Costa, epitomizes the internationally renowned style that is modern Brazil. Large quantities of furniture were required for the buildings of what was to be Brazil's new capital city. Rodrigues's designs are characteristically based on the use of traditional local materials, with a combination of native woods and leather giving his work a sensual, natural, and comfortable look. An example of Rodrigues's most famous creation, the "Poltrona Mole" (meaning "soft armchair") designed in 1957, which is also known as the "Sheriff" lounge chair, is part of the permanent collection of the Museum of Modern Art in New York – testament to the verve and character of post-war Brazilian design.

Japan

Design in post-war Japan was highly influenced by the need to rebuild the country's economy quickly. Using American money to finance this expansion, the model was similar to that used in post-war Germany, with cheap consumer goods enjoying no cohesive design policy being mass-produced to penetrate foreign markets.

Japan's design identity grew in confidence during the 1950s and 1960s, with furniture and industrial designers such as Katsuhei Toyoguchi (1905–91), Isamu Kenmochi (1912–71), and Inui Saburou (1911–91) tackling the juxtaposition between European expectations and traditional Japanese design in their work.

Toyoguchi, a pioneer of Japanese modern design is, along with many of his contemporaries, lesser-known in the West. However, much of the work of Japanese designers from the period has since reached an iconic status. A good example is the sensuous "Butterfly Stool" designed in 1956 by Sori Yanagi (1915-2011), which brought the purity of the Japanese aesthetic into the Western home. Yanagi's curvaceous stool, evocative of a shrine gate, won an award at the Milan Triennale in 1957.

A c.1950 Japanese skyscraper lamp box. 48.75in (124cm) high, **H**

Before the 20th century, chairs were not often found in Japanese homes, as people usually sat on tatami matting. The low "Spoke" chair, designed by Katsuhei Toyoguchi in 1963, adapts Western conventions to suit local customs. 32.5in (83cm) high, **L**

A low table designed by Inui Saburou in 1959. 47.5 in (121cm) wide, **H**

This traditional Japanese low table designed by Isamu Kenmochi in 1968 has a slight indentation or "mizukaeshi" (water embankment) around the edge of the table top. 55in (140cm) wide, **N**

A "Ply" chair, beech with maple veneer, designed by Inui Saburou, in 1960. 28.5in (72.5cm) high, **I**

Made of blocks of cedar, the "Kashiwado" chair, designed by Isamu Kenmochi in 1961, is named after a famous sumo wrestler. 24.75in (63cm), **O**

A "Butterfly" stool designed by Soir Yanagi in 1956, beech with rosewood veneer. 15in (38.5cm) high, **E**

The geometric "Murai" stool was designed by Reiko Tanabe in 1961. 14in (36cm) high, **F**

Glass

Introduction

Unlike other materials and manufacturing techniques, glass and the methods used to turn it into a commercial product or artistic statement did not change significantly in the decades after World War II. What did change were the ways that the material and the often ancient techniques were used.

The post-war period saw three key centres of innovation in glass design: Scandinavia, the Italian island of Murano, and Czechoslovakia. Secondary centres were West and East Germany, Great Britain, and the United States, together with other European countries including France and the Netherlands.

The post-war design revolution was led by a number of key glass factories, many of which were long-established companies with their own traditions and large market share. However, as with many other high points in design history, other companies were founded to take advantage of the boom in the market caused by a new style becoming widely desirable. In addition, the post-war period saw an increase in a phenomenon that had begun in the late 19th century: the employment of designers, who collaborated with the glass blowers. Many of these, particularly in Sweden and on Murano, were freelance or consultant designers who also worked in other fields such as architecture, painting, and graphic design, and contributed designs to several manufacturers. This ensured that companies innovated constantly, producing work that was fashionable, in tune with changing tastes in interiors, and likely to be popular with a growing urban class with more disposable income and a largely positive view of the future.

As a market clearly existed for these new products, once a new design proved to be a commercial success, competitors would spring into action and release their own mass-produced version of it. Or they would analyze and identify the elements that made a piece successful and adapt them. Most glass of this period is unmarked, which causes many problems for collectors, researchers, and historians today.

Modern and abstract art produced since the early 20th century was a key influence on designs of this time, and in the 1960s, Pop art also contributed to the melting pot of ideas. These influences manifested themselves in glass in vibrant colours and with strong geometric patterns – polar opposites of the richly embellished traditional glass that had gone before, and was still popular with more conservative parts of society at the time.

Top: An early 1950s Italian Fratelli Toso "Kiku" murrine vase, designed by Ermanno Toso. Although an ancient technique, the use of murrines has been updated with bright colours and star-like patterns on a classic, yet modern-looking, form. 10.25in (26cm) high, **R**

Bottom: A 1960s Swedish Kosta ovoid vase, with spiralling internal threads, designed by Vicke Lindstrand. Balanced, harmonious colours and forms became recurrent themes in Scandinavian glass of this era. 6.25in (16cm) high, **D**

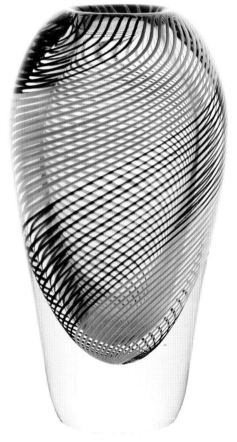

Modernism and the Art Deco style that was fashionable in the decades before the war were two further influences, primarily affecting form: the lines of vessels became cleaner and simpler, but colour and pattern – or the lack thereof – were also affected. The functionality of a piece was a key aspect of many designs, particularly those produced in Germany and Scandinavia where designers wanted to produce good design with visual appeal at an affordable price.

Conversely, and perhaps provoked by the horrors of a machine-led war, nature also proved to be a strong inspiration, particularly during the 1950s. Organic, curving, and asymmetric forms that were completely different from the Art Nouveau style of the turn of the century dominated this period, often in colours inspired by the landscape.

Three 1960s–70s Finnish Riihimäen Lasi Oy mould-spun vases. Created by a team of Finnish designers, they were part of a range of affordable, colourful, geometrically modern vases exported to Britain and the rest of Europe. 11in (28cm) high, **B** each

Italy

Left: A 1950s–60s A.Ve.M. "Bizzantina" glass toothpick holder. This range decorated with random sections of coloured canes was probably also made by other factories, and its designer is unknown. It can also be found with green or blue interiors. 2.5in (6.5cm) high **E**

Right: A Barovier & Toso "Eugeneo" jug vase, designed by Ercole Barovier c.1951. The extravagantly pulled handle and lip, as well as the gold foil inclusions on a vertically ribbed dark blue-green base, are typical of this range. 16in (41cm) high, **J**

Situated in the Venetian lagoon, the island of Murano has a long history of glassmaking. In the 13th century, glassmakers were moved from the main island of Venice to Murano in order to protect the wealthy mercantile capital city from the risk of devastation caused by fires spreading from the furnaces.

Over the next few centuries, wares produced on Murano dominated European glass, until the island's pre-eminence was challenged by George Ravenscroft's development of lead crystal in London in the late 17th century. Despite a decline in its popularity, Venetian glass endured, although styles largely stagnated, remaining centred on traditional historical forms, patterns, and techniques.

The origins of the post-war revolution in style can be traced to the early 20th century, when a number of progressive glass manufacturers employed designers who either adapted old designs or produced new ones, many of which fitted in with the prevalent Art Deco style. Good examples include Carlo Scarpa (1906–78), Napoleone Martinuzzi (1892–1977), and Vittorio Zecchin (1878–1947). The highly skilled workforce on Murano was critical to these early successes, as these craftsmen were able to translate new designs into reality in the furnace. This period also saw the founding of a number of new factories which were ready to take the glass world by storm after the war.

The rebirth of Murano glass after World War II came about in a surprisingly short amount of time, over the course of a ten-year period from the late 1940s to the late 1950s. Designs produced in subsequent decades continued to be innovative, but followed the core themes laid down during this era. A key aspect of this revolution was that fine artists, architects, sculptors, and graphic designers were again taken on as designers. Many were freelance and worked at a number of different factories during their careers before a second generation of designers began to take over in the 1970s. Some companies even employed designers from outside Italy, with manufacturers such as Venini bringing in the talents of key designers from Scandinavian countries. This injected Murano glass with a further, very different aesthetic. Free from any preconceptions about (Venetian) glass design, these designers breathed new life into the industry, drawing on disparate themes from the developing modern design and art world around them.

Modern art produced in Europe since the 1910s was a key influence, both in terms of colour and pattern. Colours erupted in a rainbow of vibrancy, and were often contrasted against each other. Patterns became more abstract and were often executed in a painterly or sculptural manner, as with the influential *sommerso* technique. Surface decoration – always a key strength of Murano, where hot-working skills were at the forefront of production – blossomed in experimental variety.

Forms also changed: the fussy complexity of historical shapes, typically embellished with many additional details such as fish-shaped stems or curving and twisted floral or foliate applications, were abandoned. They were replaced by simple, clean-lined forms, many of them based on geometric shapes such as rectangles, ovals, or cones, that served to display the combination of colours and patterns to maximum effect. Some designs, like those produced by Ercole Barovier (1889–1974), consciously echoed historic and traditional designs but updated them in a strongly modern idiom.

However, due to a lasting demand for the glass on which Murano had built its reputation, traditional and historic designs continued to be produced throughout the post-war years. The core methods used to manufacture these designs, many of which date back to Roman times, did not change either. Traditional techniques, such as the application of murrines or canes containing coloured threads, or the ancient technique of casing or layering glass, formed the core of the production process, but the colours used were new, as were the forms and patterns to which they were applied. As the skilled glassmakers were fluent in the use of these techniques, the resulting glass was as high in quality as it was entirely novel in look and feel.

Left: An Aureliano Toso "Mezza filigrana bianca nera" vase, designed by Dino Martens, c.1954. The name refers to the dark purple (almost black) and white canes with aventurine inclusions that cover the colourless body. 8in (20.5cm) high, **L**

Right: A Vetreria Vistosi "Pulcino" (chick) figurine with murrine eyes, designed by Alessandro Pianon in 1961. This colourful, whimsical bird is typical of the sense of fun and positivity that characterizes some post-war Murano designs. 8.6in (21.5cm) high, **M**

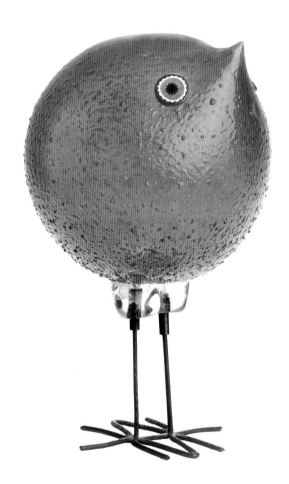

Italy

This revolution in glass also reflected a renewed positivity across Italy, and indeed most of Europe, following the privations and devastation of war. Much of the country returned to the crafts of old, which were updated and adapted for the modern age. Workers rallied to revive declining industries and create new and appealing products that could be sold to support the growing Italian economy.

On the home front, the often whimsical designs in cheerful colours brightened up rooms and lives, and perfectly matched the modern furniture designs being produced across Europe. As the 1950s progressed, these furniture designs in turn affected glass design on Murano. The work of these innovative designers and the leading glass manufacturers that supported them was exhibited around the world at international exhibitions. Exposed to the public and the wider design community, many of these pieces became new global design icons, and their style was frequently copied by other glass companies. This success inspired smaller, less well-known factories on Murano to copy the work of the leading designers of the day. Typically smaller in size as well as lower in quality, these imitations flooded the market and were exported all over the world as inexpensive ornaments for modern interiors or were sold to tourists as souvenirs.

Combined with the enormous output of the industry they inspired, the ground-breaking work of these far-sighted designers put Murano glass firmly at the forefront of European glass design by the late 1950s. This commercial and artistic success was built upon over the following decades to such an extent that by the late 20th century, Murano glass could almost be said to have become a hotly desirable global brand.

Opposite, left: A Fratelli Toso "Stellato" vase, designed by Pollio Perelda in 1953. As well as changing in colour and style, over time traditional murrines changed in size from the tiny millefiori to larger panels of glass, as with the star-shaped murrines in this vase. 10.5in (26cm) high, **O**

Opposite, right: A late 1950s Seguso Vetri d'Arte "Pesce" (fish) sommerso sculpture, designed by Flavio Poli. Highly stylized and abstracted animal forms by great designers were widely copied and imitated by smaller factories to sell as inexpensive souvenirs or ornaments. 17in (43cm) high, **L**

Left: A 1960s Vetreria Artistica Archimede Seguso conical vase, designed by Archimede Seguso. The rectilinear pattern echoes the geometric form and recalls abstract art of the time, but was made using centuries-old techniques. 8.5in (21cm) high, **R**

Right: A Venini & C. "A Fasce" (banded) rectangular vase, designed by Fulvio Bianconi c.1953. This popular range was produced in different colours and many shapes, including decanters and tall stoppered bottles. 10in (24.5cm) high, **U**

Venini & C.

Founded in 1921 by the Venetian antiques dealer Giacomo Cappellin (1887–1968) and Milanese lawyer Paolo Venini (1895–1959), Venini & C. became a major force in the post-war period. The company's success lay in Venini's desire to employ a number of leading artists as designers, which included architects Gio Ponti (1891–1979) and Carlo Scarpa (1906–78) as well as Carlo's son, furniture designer and architect Tobia Scarpa (b. 1935) and graphic designer Fulvio Bianconi (see "A Closer Look"). The company also hired foreign designers, such as the Finnish industrial designer Tapio Wirkkala (1915–85). Paolo Venini collaborated closely with these designers, sometimes adapting their designs, and also produced designs of his own. The company revived and updated a number of traditional techniques, mostly focusing on vibrant colours and surface decoration.

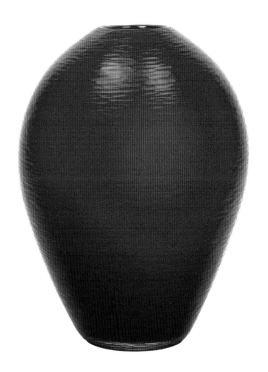

A Venini & C. "Battuto" ovoid vase, designed by Carlo Scarpa in 1940. Battuto is an Italian word used to describe beaten metal. The exterior of the orange-red, colourless-cased body is decorated with many horizontal cuts of different sizes. 8in (20.5cm) high, **M**

A Venini & C. "Fazzoletto" (handkerchief) vase, designed by Fulvio Bianconi and Paolo Venini in 1949. An iconic design of post-war Murano, which was produced and copied in many different colours and patterns. This form captures a handkerchief falling through the air. 10in (25.5cm) high, **I**

A Venini & C. "Capello del Doge" (Doge's hat) doppio incalmo glass sculpture, designed by American glass designer Thomas Stearns in 1962. Resembling the hat worn by Venice's elected ruler, this ground-breaking design was too difficult to put into production. 5.25in (13.5cm) wide, **U**

A pair of Venini & C. "Gallo E Gallini" figurines of a rooster and a hen, designed by Fulvio Bianconi c.1950. The opaque white glass bodies are decorated with applied multicoloured threads, stripes, and pulled features. Bianconi's human figurines tend to be more popular than his animal figurines. 7.25in (18cm) high, **L**

A Venini & C. "Occhi" (eyes) bottle vase, designed by Tobia Scarpa in 1959. The colourless glass body is decorated with tightly packed murrines with colourless glass centres and red borders. This successful design is still produced today. 8.5in (22cm) high, **L**

Fulvio Bianconi

The "Pezzato" (patches) range was designed between 1950 and 1951, and was exhibited to great acclaim at the Milan Triennale exhibition in 1951.

The design can be found on different shapes and in different colour combinations, each with its own name. The colours and design echo modern abstract paintings, as well as stained glass windows.

A colourless glass body is first blown and then rolled over panels of coloured glass, which stick to the hot body and create a patchwork effect. The body is then blown to its final form.

*A Venini "Pezzato" glass vase, by Fulvio Bianconi. 9in (22.8cm) high. **R***

Fulvio Bianconi (1915–96) joined Venini in 1947, after working for a number of major Italian publishers as a graphic designer. Over the next two decades he became one of the glass manufacturer's most important designers, and some of his designs are still produced today. Forms and patterns tend to be bold and simple, relying on strong, contrasting colours. Apart from the influential "Fazzoletto" bowl (see opposite), his most important and notable design is perhaps the "Pezzato" range (see above). Others include the vertically striped "Fasce Verticali" vases, and the "Fasce Orrizontale" range with its broad horizontal bands. Bianconi also designed whimsical figurines, some of them based on characters from the *commedia dell'arte*.

Barovier & Toso

Left: A Barovier & Toso "Crepuscolo" lamp base, designed by Ercole Barovier c.1950. Some designs, such as "Cordonato d'Oro", were produced for long periods of time. "Crepuscolo", which contains iron wool inclusions, was first developed around 1935–6, and continued to be produced after the war. 13.5in (34cm) high, **E**

Right: A Barovier & Toso "A Spina" cylindrical vase, designed by Ercole Barovier in 1957. The simple form is overlaid with panels of opalescent white and turquoise glass, giving the pattern the appearance of herringbone weave. 11.5in (29cm) high, **N**

Barovier & Toso was formed in 1936, when the Barovier glassworks, founded in 1878 on the island of Murano, merged with the Ferro Toso glassworks, founded in 1901. The new firm's successful designs were produced by Ercole Barovier (1889–1974) and his son Angelo (b. 1927), who began working at the factory in 1947 and became a designer in 1951. Angelo took over the company from his father in 1972.

Although Ercole was particularly prolific, both father and son produced designs notable for their innovative and inventive reinterpretation of traditional techniques. Although the shape was important as regards the theme of a range, both designers focused on surface decoration. Many of their designs were complex, and they used almost every combination and type of pattern, resulting in vessels decorated with stripes, patchwork, herringbone, threading, combed effects, and criss-crossing tartans. The company also produced a number of traditional and modern lighting designs, most notably large chandeliers.

Unlike many other glass designers of this time, the Baroviers did not focus purely on modern shapes and patterns or bright colours. Many of their pieces were designed to have an ancient or primitive appearance, and were based on archaic forms and surface patterns. This retrospective look can be seen in a number of ranges, such as the "Aborigeno" range of 1951, with its randomly crackled surface and forms derived from surviving examples of Roman or Phoenician glass. Inspired by ancient glass that had been uncovered in archaeological excavations, the "Barbarico" range designed in the early 1950s pushed this theme further. The "Efeso" range of 1964, with bodies containing thousands of differently sized air bubbles and powder inclusions, has a similar feel. In some cases, the glass was textured, iridized, or treated with oxides to further give the impression of age. Unusual materials such as iron wool were sometimes also used.

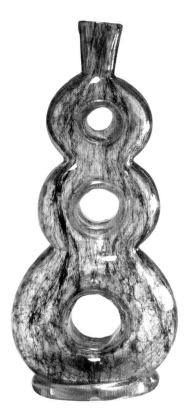

Traditional Muranese designs were echoed in the widely produced "Cordonato d'Oro" range introduced in 1950, where the bodies appear to be made up of vertically ribbed glass ropes embellished internally with fragments of sparkling gold foil. Forms are typically chunky and curving, and rims are often pulled into extravagant curls.

Despite this interest in old patterns and forms, Barovier & Toso did respond to the popular movement towards modern designs, and joined its contemporaries in updating traditional techniques in the modern idiom. Vases and bowls decorated with *zanfirico* rods were produced in vibrant colour combinations such as bright yellow, red, and green, and increasingly inventive murrines were used to create ranges such as the "Athena Cattedrale" series of 1964.

Three other highly notable ranges which echo Fulvio Bianconi's designs for Venini are "Parabolico", introduced in 1957, and "Moreschi" and "Intarsio" (which means "inlay"), both introduced in 1961. All use multicoloured panels of glass to create interesting visual effects. The pattern on "Parabolico" pieces looks as if wide panels of glass have been woven together on the surface, while "Intarsio" relies on the stunning abstract effect created by a geometric arrangement of triangular panels in a contrasting colour to the body.

Left: A Barovier & Toso "Athena Cattedrale" bottle vase, designed by Ercole Barovier in 1964. The surface of the colourless body is decorated with columns of diamond-shaped murrines, each with a complex olive green, opaque white, colourless, and blue design. 11in (27.5cm) high, **R**

Right: A Barovier & Toso "Rotellato" glass vase, designed by Ercole Barovier in 1970. The stylized floral pattern of the murrines hark back to 19th-century millefiori designs. This was one of Ercole Barovier's last designs for the company. 10.5in (27cm) high, L

Alfredo Barbini
Fratelli Toso
Seguso Vetri d'Arte

Thanks largely to the award-winning work of Flavio Poli (1900–84) at Seguso Vetri d'Arte, a glass company founded in 1933, *sommerso* (submerged) designs became one of the most influential styles on the island of Murano and beyond. Although casing had been practised for centuries, the technique was refreshed with modern, curving forms and vivid colours. The same themes lay behind the revival of the murrine technique, which became ever more abstract and colourful. This movement was championed by the painter Pollio Perelda (1915–84) at Fratelli Toso (founded in 1854), and particularly by glassmaker and designer Ermanno Toso (1903–73). After working at a number of different glass companies, Alfredo Barbini (b. 1912) opened his own in 1950, and continued to develop his experimental style.

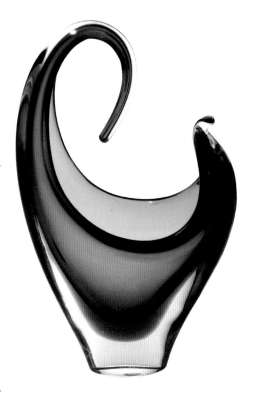

A Seguso Vetri d'Arte "Sommerso" bowl, with asymmetrically pulled and curled rim, c.1950. Exaggerated, pulled rims are common features of many 1950s–70s "sommerso" designs produced on Murano, and were formed when the glass was still molten. 11.5in (29cm) high, **L**

A Vetreria Artistica Archimede Seguso "Losanghe" vase, designed by Archimede Seguso, c.1952. After working at Seguso Vetri d'Arte, Archimede Seguso (1909–99) founded his own company in 1946. He used the "filigrana" technique frequently. 11.5in (29cm) high, **N**

A Fratelli Toso "nerox" vase, designed by Ermanno Toso c.1960. Iridescent and almost black, "nerox" glass was a speciality of Ermanno Toso and has a satin-effect finish. The multicoloured spots were applied separately. 5in (12.5cm) high, **P**

A Fratelli Toso "stellato" vase, designed by Pollio Perelda, c.1953. The colourless cylindrical body is covered with multicoloured star-shaped murrines, hence the name. 13.5in (34cm) high, **Q**

A Seguso Vetri d'Arte "sommerso" vase, designed by Flavio Poli, c.1955. The influential "sommerso" pieces Poli designed from the 1930s to the 1950s were widely copied by other factories in many colours and forms. 17.5in (44cm) high, **M**

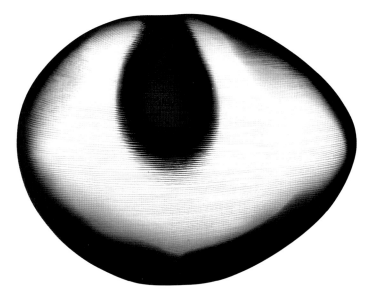

An Aureliano Toso "filigrana" vase, designed by Dino Martens, c.1956. The term "filigrana" is used to describe pieces whose surface is embellished with canes containing coloured glass threads. The technique was introduced by Venetians in the 16th century in imitation of Roman glass. The 13.5in (34cm) high, **M**

A Vetreria Alfredo Barbini "vetro pesante" (heavy glass) vase, designed by Alfredo Barbini, c.1962. The surface of this heavily cased "sommerso" vase is decorated with densely packed fine cuts, in a finish known as "inciso". 8.75in (22cm) wide, **M**

Dino Martens

The landmark "Oriente" range was launched at the 1952 Venice Biennale, and is much sought after today.

This shape number, 5139, was one of the earliest designs produced for the range. Compared to other designs in the range it is unusual for its symmetry.

Many techniques are combined – copper aventurine inclusions appear in the design, as do random sections of zanfirico cane.

The broad splashes of opaque clashing colours have been chosen and applied to resemble paint, and are hard to achieve successfully.

The large dark violet and white sunburst shape is a murrine that has been applied to the surface.

An Aureliano Toso "Oriente" carafe vase, designed by Dino Martens in 1952. 14in (33cm) high. **P.**

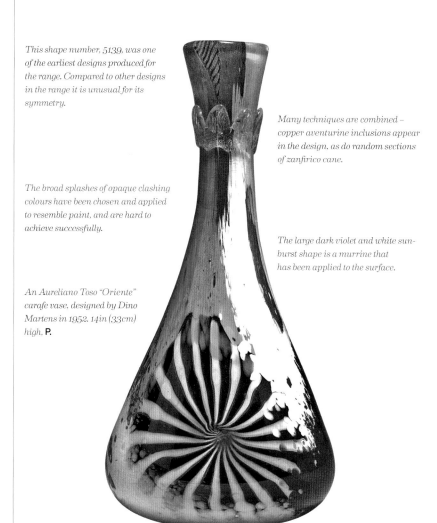

Dino Martens (1894–1970) originally trained at the Academy of Fine Art in Florence before turning to glassmaking in the 1920s. In 1939, he became artistic director at Aureliano Toso, and between 1946 and 1963, he produced a number of designs that are considered daring in terms of their asymmetric shapes and exuberant, colourful patterns. Utilizing a variety of traditional techniques in a bold new manner, Martens drew on his artistic experience and treated glass like paint. His designs, which first created a stir at the 1948 Venice Biennale, were much-imitated but never bettered. He also produced designs for Salviati that had extravagant handles and spouts, and harked back to traditional Venetian serpent-stemmed vessels.

Arte Vetraria Muranese
Cenedese
Vistosi

Most of the designers at Arte Vetraria Muranese (A.Ve.M), founded in 1932, were initially glassblowers but subsequently became designers. These included co-founders Giulio Radi (1895–1952) and Emilio Nason (1891–1959), with the sons of other co-founders – the painter Giorgio Ferro (b. 1931) and Luciano Ferro (1925–72) – also contributing designs during the 1950s and the 1960s respectively. Founded in 1946, Vetreria Gino Cenedese is best known for its lighting designs and the "sommerso" pieces created by Antonia da Ros (b. 1936) from the 1950s to the 1970s, many of which had block-like forms containing layers of different tones of one colour. More experimental designs were produced by artist Luigi Scarpa Croce (1901–67) and Fulvio Bianconi. Founded in 1945, the Vistosi glassworks also employed freelance designers, although some 1960s designs were produced by Gino Vistosi, the founder's son.

A Vetreria Gino Cenedese "sommerso" fish sculpture, designed by Antonio da Ros, c.1950. Cenedese became known for its "sommerso" designs, most of which were produced by Antonio da Ros who became artistic director of the firm in 1958. 14in (34.5cm) long, **L**

A 1950s–60s Murano glass triple-cased "sommerso" swan sculpture. This elegant sculpture is a better example of the tens of thousands of figurines churned out by glassworks on Murano who copied the work of innovative and progressive designers. 14.5in (37cm) high, **D**

A Vetreria Vistosi vase with a band of coloured murrines, designed by Peter Pelzel in 1962. Pelzel was one of a number of freelance designers employed by the company during the 1960s. This design was produced on a variety of different forms. 8.75in (22cm) high, **E**

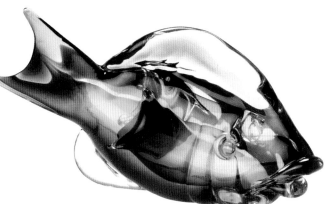

A Vistosi "pulcino" (chick) bird sculpture, designed by Alessandro Pianon in 1961. Freelance designer Pianon (1931–84) produced a range of four stylized bird figurines, all of which were blown in geometric shapes and decorated with canes or murrines. 12in (30cm) high, **N**

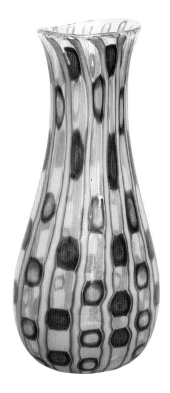

An A.Ve.M "anse volante" (flying handle) vase, designed by Giorgio Ferro in 1952. This range of jugs and vases, all with extravagant handles, was launched at the 1952 Venice Biennale. Produced in dark red or green, all had iridescent surfaces. 8.5in (22cm) high, **L**

An A.Ve.M baluster vase, designed by Anzolo Fuga in 1960. Anzolo Fuga (1914–98), who worked for A.Ve.M. from 1955 to 1968, produced eccentric, artistic designs comprising carefully arranged canes, murrines, and opaque white and coloured glass. 17in (43cm) high, **L**

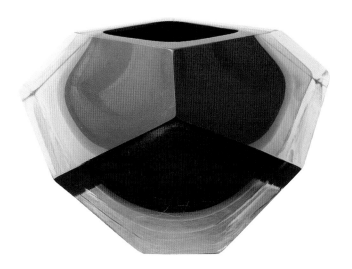

A Vetreria Gino Cenedese horse sculpture, designed by Antonio Da Ros in 1965. Like Seguso Vetri d'Arte, Cenedese produced a variety of animal figurines, which were copied, typically in smaller sizes, by many Muranese factories to sell as tourist souvenirs. 10.25in (26cm) high, **N**

A 1960s Murano glass triple-cased and cut "sommerso" ashtray. The origins of unlabelled examples may never be known – this type of piece was produced by a large number of factories on Murano. Vases and bowls of different faceted shapes can be found. 4in (10cm) high, **C**

Scandinavia

Renowned for its high quality, which resulted in superb clarity and purity, Scandinavian glass became highly influential across the world in the post-war period. Harmonic, balanced, and stylish, Scandinavian designs were almost immediately considered as important as those from Murano, and were just as highly regarded. A key inspiration throughout the period was nature, with many of the designers employed by Scandinavian factories looking to the rich and rugged landscape around them.

In general, Scandinavian glass design can be divided into three main areas, although there are overlaps and exceptions. The 1950s saw shapes take on a curving, asymmetric style, typically with chunky walls and often inspired by organic forms such as flower buds, mushrooms, and leaves. Colours were typically cool, restrained, and transparent, inspired by the icy Scandinavian environment. The designs Per Lütken (1916–98) produced for Denmark's Holmegaard factory (see page 122) are good examples, as are the landmark designs manufactured by Orrefors (see page 120) in Sweden.

In the 1960s, this organic style gave way to more geometric forms that were executed in vivid colours like orange and red, such as the pieces designed for Finland's Riihimäen Lasi Oy. Towards the end of the decade and into the 1970s, glass with textured surfaces became popular. Created using moulds, these textures could be abstract or inspired by natural surfaces, such as those of rock, ice, or bark.

Together with Orrefors, the leading Scandinavian glassworks of the time was Kosta, founded in Sweden in 1742. The company saw renewed commercial success after the appointment of Elis Bergh (1881–1954) as a designer in 1929. She was replaced in 1950 by Vicke Lindstrand (1904–83) who had already enjoyed a successful career at competitor Orrefors and went on to become one of Kosta's most prolific and popular designers. Like most Scandinavian glass factories, Kosta benefitted from employing talented, often independent, artists as designers. As well as those mentioned in the captions on this page, these included Tyra Lundgren (1897–1979) and stage designer Sven Erik Skawonius (1908–81), whose pre-war designs continued to be produced after the war.

In 1964, Kosta merged with competitor Boda, who had been acquired by another factory, Åfors, just after the war. The group's managing director was Erik Rosén, a young man who continued to put his progressive ideas into practice at the newly formed company. He was responsible for employing husband-and-wife team Göran (b. 1933) and Ann Wärff (b. 1937) in 1964, and silversmith Sigurd Persson (b. 1914) in 1968. The Wärffs dominated Kosta in terms of design, and presaged the studio glass movement by injecting spontaneity into their designs and production processes. They also used etching techniques to reveal underlying layers on vessels that had been cased a number of times, using colour in a painterly, expressive manner. In 1978, glass designer Bengt Edenfalk (b. 1924) joined the company from the Skruf glassworks, and produced a number of designs with subtly coloured, cased layers.

Orrefors

Although Orrefors had been largely eclipsed by its rival Kosta (see page 118) before the war, the post-war period saw the company, which was founded in 1898, rise to a pre-eminent position in Scandinavian glass design. The foundations for this success were laid in the 1920s and 1930s with the award-winning designs of Simon Gate (1883–1945) and Edward Hald (1883–1980). After the war, these predominantly Classical or Art Deco forms with cut, engraved, or enamelled designs were replaced with new curving and organic, yet modern, forms.

Two landmark examples were the "Tulpanglas" (tulip glass) goblet, designed by Nils Landberg (1906–84) in 1954, and the instantly recognizable "Äpplet" (apple) display object designed by Ingeborg Lundin (1921–92) in 1955. Both were shown at the Milan Triennale in 1957, with the "Tulpanglas" winning a gold medal. The inspiration from nature is evident, and this continued to be an influential theme during the 1950s. Gently curved, often bud-like, forms were frequently cut or engraved with stylized figures as well as floral or foliate designs, or were produced in muted colours cased in colourless glass.

Landberg and Lundin were part of an influential team of designers that also included Vicke Lindstrand (1904–83, see page 124), Sven Palmqvist (1906–84), and, from 1959, Gunnar Cyrén (b. 1931). The team also produced designs for tableware that, like their decorative wares, relied on the clarity and quality of the glass itself, the clear lines of simple forms, and muted colours. Cyrén is best known for his 1960s "Popglas" range of goblets made, unusually for Orrefors, in brightly coloured opaque glass.

Innovative and technically complex designs introduced before the war continued to be produced. The most important of these was "Graal", developed from 1916 onwards by Gate and master glassblower Knut Bergqvist. "Graal" ingeniously combines the techniques of casing, engraving, and blowing to create a unique design. A small blank was first cased with several layers of differently coloured glass. Once cool, this was engraved, cut, or etched with designs so that the underlying colours were revealed. It was then reheated and cased with colourless glass, before being blown outwards into the desired form. Each piece is unique due to the production process, and most designs were not repeated. Hald's popular "Fiskegraal" (Fish Graal) design of 1937 is unusual, as it went into serial production, and was produced into the late 1980s.

The "Graal" technique was used from the 1940s onwards in designs by Hald, Lundin, and Eva Englund (1937–98). "Ariel", developed in 1936 by glassblower Gustav Bergqvist and designers Edvin Öhrström (1906–94) and Lindstrand, is related to "Graal". However, instead of being etched or engraved, the blank was sandblasted with a design before being cased and blown out into form. This resulted in a more fluid appearance to the pattern, due to the air trapped in the sandblasted cavities under the outer layer.

These techniques were added to by Palmqvist with his "Kraka" and "Ravenna" ranges, which were developed in 1944 and 1948 respectively, and put into serial production. Emulating stained glass windows, "Ravenna" was made by fusing differently coloured glass panels together before sandblasting them to create cavities. These were filled with coloured glass powder, and the piece was then reheated and blown into a mould. "Kraka" is similar to "Graal", but the pattern consists of a net of fine lines set against a graduated coloured ground.

The designers employed by Orrefors maintained the company's success in the mid 20th century, and their designs became highly influential not just in Scandinavia, but around the world. Pieces made by Orrefors typically bear engraved marks on the base. A series of letters and numbers found next to the company's name can help to identify the designer, the method of production or decoration, and the design number.

Holmegaard

Founded in Denmark in 1825, Holmegaard initially produced bottles and utilitarian wares. In the first half of the 20th century, the company's designers included Oluf Jensen and Orla Juul Nielsen, whose tableware designs were exhibited at the Paris Exposition in 1925. Other designs manufactured by Holmegaard were largely traditional, or derived from the production of other factories.

Holmegaard's most important and influential designer of the post-war era was Per Lütken (1916–98), who joined the company in 1942 and went on to produce thousands of highly successful designs. His 1950s pieces are typified by curving, bud-like, and sometimes asymmetric forms inspired by nature. All were executed in cool, transparent colours, from greys and icy blues to various hues of green. The "Duckling" vase, designed in 1952, and the heart-shaped "Minuet" vase, designed in 1955, are typical of his work from this period.

Other designs for decorative and table wares were equally simple in form, comprising barrel, cylindrical, or conical forms. Usually unembellished, they relied on the simplicity of the internal and external lines, the graduated colour caused by different thicknesses of glass, and the clarity of the glass itself. Highly successful, many were produced for decades, and some are still in production today. This pared-down aesthetic was countered with the "Carnaby" range, designed by Lütken from 1968. Built from geometric elements such as cylinders and ovals, forms were executed in vibrant colours such as red, blue, or yellow over an opaque white base, which gave them the appearance of plastic.

Lütken also produced a number of unique exhibition pieces and ranges that can almost be classed as studio glass. Although executed to a design, each piece is unique due to the way it is made. A notable early design was the "Orchid", designed in 1958. A bulbous cased bubble of molten glass was pierced with a pin and the resulting rush of hot air created an aperture, echoed by the attenuated, pulled rim. In 1969, Lütken devised the "Lava" range of vases and bottles, which was manufactured into the late 1970s. Produced in brown-red, and blue and white, the streaky pattern was unique to each piece, as was the final form, which was created using a mould made from wet clay.

Jacob Bang (1899–1965), who joined Holmegaard in 1927, was another key designer. Bang left the company in 1941 to design ceramics. He returned to Holmegaard's sister company Kastrup in 1957, and further developed the clarity of line and form found in his successful pre-war "Viol" and "Primula" ranges of tableware. The results can be seen in Bang's clean-lined, austere design for vases, bowls, and tableware. His son Michael (b. 1944) began working with Holmegaard in 1968, and is best known for his 1970s "Palette" and "Napoli" ranges, which are similar in appearance to Lütken's "Carnaby" range, but were produced in different shapes and as kitchenware.

Opposite, left: A Holmegaard "Carnaby" range vase, designed by Per Lütken in 1968. This mould-blown range of fifteen vases and a pitcher was produced from 1969 to 1976, and met with great success. Rims are rounded, not machine-cut. 12in (30.5cm) high, **G**

Opposite, centre: A Holmegaard "Aqua" blue "Minuet" vase, designed by Per Lütken in 1952. This vase is also known as the "heart" vase due to its shape, and was produced in greys, greens, and blues from 1955 to 1976. 7in (18cm) high, **E**

Opposite, right: A Holmegaard light-green "Duckling" vase, designed by Per Lütken in 1950. Produced from 1952 to 1976 in a range of sizes and colours, these were nicknamed "Naebvas" (beak vases). 8in (20cm) high, **A**

Below, left: A Holmegaard "Sapphire" blue cylinder vase, designed by Per Lütken in 1966. These popular and practical cylindrical vases were produced in large quantities in different sizes and colours. 6.75in (17cm) high, **B**

Below, right: A Kastrup amber-brown "Gulvvase", designed by Otto Brauer in 1962. Glassblower Brauer's popular and widely produced mould-blown bottle vases were based on a shorter form, originally designed by Per Lütken in 1958. 12in (305cm) high, **B**

Vicke Lindstrand

(1904–83)

Victor Emanuel Lindstrand, known as Vicke, studied art and illustration in Gothenburg as well as in Italy and France. He joined the design department at Orrefors in 1928, having been hired to help relieve the workload of lead designers Edward Hald and Simon Gate. His work was almost immediately successful, and in the 1930s he produced a large number of modern, Art-Deco-inspired designs that were cut, engraved, or enamelled onto simple vase forms. Lindstrand frequently made use of the entire body, applying designs all over the exterior of a vessel in order to give the design a three-dimensional effect. His forms were often asymmetric, while his highly stylized designs, which focused on the natural world and the human figure in particular, all show a strong understanding of line, reflecting his background and training. His best-known work from this period includes the "Pearl Divers" range dating from 1931–5, as well as the contribution he made to the development of the "Ariel" technique in 1936 (see page 120).

In 1940, Lindstrand left Orrefors to design ceramics for Upsala-Ekeby and Karlskrona, but returned to glass in 1951, when he joined Kosta as chief designer and art director. There, he continued to produce and develop the stylized designs for which he had become celebrated at Orrefors. He frequently combined different techniques on a single piece, and also made use of internal threads to create abstract patterns, typically on thickly cased, gently curving forms.

Top: A Kosta vase, finely engraved with a spiderweb hanging between reeds, designed by Vicke Lindstrand. The stylized natural theme and asymmetric form are hallmarks of Lindstrand's style. 15.75in (40cm) high, **D**

Below left: A Kosta "Ariel" vase, with an abstract geometric pattern, designed by Vicke Lindstrand in 1960. The pioneering "Graal" and "Ariel" techniques were later adopted by other factories, including those outside Scandinavia. 6in (14.5cm) high, **M**

Below right: A late 1950s Kosta vase with an internal fine net pattern, designed by Vicke Lindstrand. The fine threads are applied over the graduated blue to green body, which is then cased in colourless glass. 9in (23cm) high, **G**

Opposite: A Kosta "Oktober" vase, engraved with stylized trees, designed by Vicke Lindstrand in 1951. The pattern is engraved all over the exterior of the transparent body, giving the scene a sense of perspective when viewed. 9.5in (24cm) high, **L**

Riihimaki
Nuutajärvi Nöstjo

Riihimäen Lasi Oy, known as Riihimaki, was founded in Finland in 1910. From the 1930s onwards, the company held a series of competitions to recruit a talented team of designers including Helena Tynell (b. 1918) in 1946, Nanny Still (b. 1926) in 1949, and Tamara Aladin (b. 1932) in 1959. In the late 1960s and the 1970s, they designed a wide range of mould-blown vases that are typified by bright, strong colours and geometric forms. Successful and exported across Europe, some of these vessels had textured surfaces. Nuutajärvi Nöstjö, another Finnish glassworks, benefitted from the largely austere geometric designs of Kaj Franck (1911–89), as well as the designs by Gunnel Nyman (1909–48) and Oiva Toikka (b. 1931).

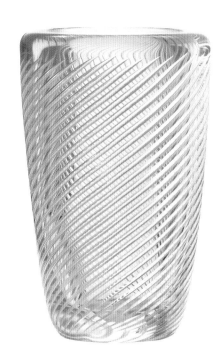

A Nuutajärvi Nostjö vase containing rows of elongated trapped air bubbles, designed by Kaj Franck in 1953. Franck's art glass was more dynamic and challenging to make than his austere tableware ranges. 3.25in (8cm) high, **C**

A Riihimäen Lasi Oy vase, no.1472, designed by Tamara Aladin in 1967. This design was part of a mass-produced range of mould-blown vases made in many bold colours from 1968 to 1976. 9.75in (25cm) high, **B**

A 1960s Riihimäen Lasi Oy cased yellow vase, no.1379, design attributed to Tamara Aladin. This was produced for the mainland European market. 8in (20cm) high, **A**

A Riihimäen Lasi Oy blue "Safari" textured vase, no.1495, designed by Tamara Aladin in 1970. Due to the texture, this was machine-blown into a mould, rather than spun. 10in (25cm) high, **A**

A late 1960s–70s Aseda vase, with dark blue powder and bubble inclusions, designed by Bo Borgström. Founded in Sweden in 1947, Aseda closed in 1977. Ceramicist Borgström was chief designer from 1961. 7in (17.5cm) high, **B**

A Strömbergshyttan vase, engraved with deer grazing in a glade. Strömbergshyttan operated in Sweden from 1933 to 1979. Designers included Gerda Strömberg, Rune Strand, and Gunnar Nylund 12in (30.5cm) high, **E**

A Ruda Glasbruk mould-blown "Kobalt" vase, designed by Göte Augustssen in the 1960s. Ruda operated from 1910 to 1972, with Augustssen as designer from 1947. 6.5in (16.5cm) high, **A**

A Nuutajärvi Notsjö "Hourglass" vase, no. kf245, designed by Kaj Franck in 1956. Made from 1956 to 1969 in yellow, lilac, brown, blue, and green, these vases are often mistaken for candleholders. 6.75in (17cm) high, **C**

A Riihimäen Lasi Oy mould-blown vase from the "Fossil" range, designed by Helena Tynell. Unusually taking its inspiration from natural history rather than the drawing board and geometry set, the "Fossil" range is rare. 6.25in (16cm) high, **C**

A Riihimaën Lasi Oy large "Kasperi" vase, designed by Erkkitapio Siiroinen in 1970. Siiroinen (1944–96) joined the company in 1968, and produced a number of designs with moulded protrusions. 12in (30.5cm) high, **C**.

Iittala

Founded in Finland in 1881, Iittala became one of the most important Scandinavian glass factories of the post-war period. The lead designers were Timo Sarpaneva (see "A Closer Look"), and Tapio Wirkkala (1915–85). Their designs were heavily inspired by the landscape around them, from icy fjords to rock and bark, flora and fauna.

Key designs by Wirkkala include the "Kantarelli" (chanterelle) vase of 1946, which was inspired by fungi and won the Grand Prix at the Milan Triennale in 1951, the "Jäkälä" (lichen) vase of 1950, and the attenuated "Varsanjalka" (foal's foot) vase of 1947, with its finely engraved vertical lines. He also produced textured designs, including the "Ultima Thule" range of tableware, as well as a range for Finlandia vodka.

Good

An Iittala bowl, no.3132, designed by Tapio Wirkkala in 1955. The asymmetric body is cut with fine lines, and is typical of 1950s Scandinavian glass in terms of its colour and form. 4in (10cm) high, **C**

Better

An Iittala footed bowl, no.3523, designed by Tapio Wirkkala in 1951. Cut with fine vertical lines, and made from 1951 to 1960, this bowl was inspired by an open flower or toadstool. 9in (23cm) diam, **F**

The "Finlandia" range was developed by Timo Sarpaneva in 1964, and was initially made using moulds lined with real bark. When the molten glass was blown into the mould, it took on the texture of the bark lining

As these wooden moulds were effectively destroyed after repeated use, textured metal moulds soon replaced them for serial commercial production.

The level of texture on this example is excellent, being crisp and highly varied. Combined with the colour, the bark pattern also recalls a block of ice.

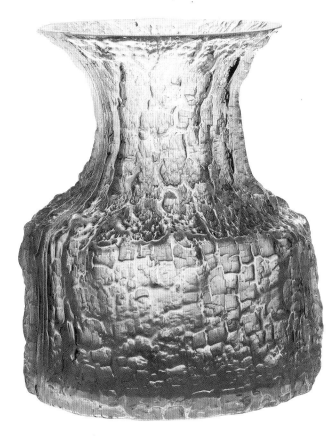

This range was inspirational for the textured glass design of the late 1960s -1970s.

An Iittala "Finlandia" vase, no.7751, designed by Timo Sarpaneva in 1964. 7in (17.5cm) high, **I**

Timo Sarpaneva (1948–2005) studied graphic design in Helsinki and went on to produce designs in almost every discipline including glass, ceramics, textiles, lighting, and metals. In 1948, he joined Iittala, where he produced hundreds of designs, some of them winning international awards. His most notable designs include the curving "Orkidea" (orchid) sculptural object of 1953, the similarly curving and cased "Lansetti" (lancet) sculptural object of 1952, which won a gold medal at the Milan Triennale in 1954, and his mass-produced "Festivo" range of textured candlesticks, introduced in 1967. He also designed the coloured and clean-lined "i-line" range of mould-blown tableware, and the highly influential textured "Finlandia" range (see above).

Best

An Iittala "Savoy" or "Aalto" vase, designed by Alvar Aalto in 1936. Iittala's rise to international prominence in the early 20th century was mainly due to the Modernist architects and furniture designers Alvar and Aino Aalto. 6in (15cm) high, **H**

Czechoslovakia

Below, left: A spherical vessel of cut, sandblasted, and polished dark green optical glass, designed and made by František Vízner. This simple, balanced form is typical of the studio glass works produced by Vízner from 1977 onwards. 5.75in (14.5cm) diam, **N**

Below, centre: A Skrdlovice vase, no.7410, designed by František Vízner in 1974. Produced in at least three sizes, this design has an industrial, monumental feel. This form recurs in Vízner's work for Skrdlovice at the time. 7.5in (19cm) high, **E**

Below, right: A 1970s Prachen amber vase, with applied blue prunts stamped with stylized floral motifs, designed by Josef Hospodka in 1969. The prunts appear green due to the transmitted light through the yellow-amber body. 9.75in (25cm) high, **B**

Opposite, left: A Mstisov "Harmony" range elliptical bowl with blue trails over a colourless cased green body, designed by František Zemek in 1959. Typical of Zemek's asymmetric, organic forms, this scarce range is similar to designs produced on Murano. 11.5in (29.5cm) long, **C**

Opposite, right: A late 1960s–70s Borské Sklo vase, designed by Pavel Hlava in 1967, with colourless casing. This undulating, warped design was probably made by blowing the glass into a modified wire cage. Hlava's studio glass techniques were translated into factory-produced glass. 10.25in (26cm) high, **B**

Although Czechoslovakia was shattered by World War II, the historic Bohemian glass industry was revived almost immediately by the country's new Communist government. Factories and educational institutions were brought under central control, and were rebuilt, enlarged, and modernized. All glass designers were trained thoroughly in the practical and technical aspects of glassmaking allowing them to work across many categories and techniques, from cut or pressed wares to blown glass. The new regime's aims were to demonstrate the success of Communism to the West and to produce and export glass to bring in valuable foreign currency. To help achieve this, glass design was represented at many international exhibitions, including the World's Fairs held in Brussels in 1958 and Montreal in 1967.

Although art in general was strictly controlled by the state and used as propaganda, the regime did not consider glass to be a medium that could convey a social or political message. As such, glass artists were free to pursue an otherwise banned modern, abstract style in their work. This unique situation led to a rebirth of glass design, which was led by progressive and experimental designers such as Stanislav Libenský (1921–2002, see pages 132-133), René Roubicek (b. 1922), and Professor Karel Stipl who taught and inspired a new wave of innovative designers, including Pavel Hlava (1924–2003), František Vízner (1936–2011), and Jiri Harcuba (b. 1928).

Czech glass of the post-war period can be divided into two clear categories: experimental and progressive designs that were produced in limited quantities or as unique art objects, and the mass-produced pieces they inspired, which were made in factories for export around the world. Most of the latter category were branded with a simple "Bohemia Glass" label by Skloexport, the Communist glass export company (*sklo* means glass), as individual artists were not promoted commercially abroad by the state.

Pressed glass designs became highly commercially successful, and are often grouped together as "Sklo Union", the name of the group of factories that made them. Key designers included František Vízner, František Pecený (1920–77), Rudolf Jurnikl (b. 1928), and Vladislav Urban (b. 1937).

Second to pressed glass in terms of both quantity produced and commercial success were designs blown and worked at the furnace, which were largely a new departure for Czechoslovakia. Away from the unique masterworks, a number of key factories and designers are particularly notable. In terms of blown and furnace-worked glass, these designers include František Zemek (1913–60) at Mstisov, Miroslav Klinger (1922–99) at Železný Brod Sklo (ZBS), and Josef Hospodka (1923–89) at Chribská, whose cased and pulled designs, produced from the mid 1950s to the 1960s, closely resemble those being made on Murano at the same time. The Škrdlovice glassworks, founded in 1940, was a hotbed of activity, employing many great designers over the period. The factory was run by Emanuel Beránek and his sons, all of whom also contributed designs. Cut glass was produced at a number of factories, including those in Nový Bor and at Podebrady. Key designers include Vladimir Zahour (b. 1925) and Josef Pravec (b. 1928), who became renowned for their modern designs.

Libenský-Brychtová

Both individually and in their working and personal partnership, glass artists Stanislav Libenský (1921–2002) and Jaroslava Brychtová (b. 1924) produced some of the most important Czech glass of the 20th century.

After training in glass design, Libenský was director of the glass school at Železný Brod before joining the faculty of the Academy of Applied Arts in Prague, where he was an influential professor from 1963 until 1987. Libenský, who had been producing delicate yet vibrant enamelled works and designs for tableware, began collaborating with Brychtová, also a teacher at Železný Brod, in 1956. The result was a cast-glass bowl moulded with a head on the exterior, which became a landmark design of its time.

By the 1960s, Libenský and Brychtová were experimenting with the optical effects of "inner space" gained by merging geometric shapes within the spatial volume of a glass form, as well as exploring stylized figural forms, often inspired by Cubism. These two themes dominated their often monumental work into the 1990s. The pair also designed large-scale architectural glass, which was exhibited in public buildings in Czechoslovakia and abroad. They participated in international exhibitions, such as the 1958 World Expo in Brussels. This won them many prizes and brought them international recognition, which increased after the fall of Communism in Czechoslovakia in 1989.

Opposite: A green glass, mould-melted, cut and polished cast-glass "Head" sculpture, designed by Stanislav Libenský and Jaroslava Brychtová in 1957, 14in (35.5cm), high. This figurative glass sculpture shows the influence of both Cubism and tribal art.

Below: A teal glass, mould-melted cast bowl, with head on its exterior, designed by Stanislav Libenský and Jaroslava Brychtová in 1956. 12in (30 cm). This landmark piece proved highly influential.

Czechoslovakia

The treatment of glass production was completely overhauled in the post-war period. Traditional complex patterns were replaced by modern, abstract patterns on simple forms. The optical effects created by the cut or moulded patterns themselves became the focus. Designs blown and worked at the furnace were similar to, and perhaps partly inspired by, those produced on Murano and in Scandinavia in terms of their colours and sculptural, often curving forms. Complex enamelled and gilded designs were produced from the late 1940s into the 1950s. Effectively modern art, they gave way to simpler, more abstract geometric patterns that could be mass-produced.

Good

Although this striking vase designed by Vladislav Urban for Rudolfová was mass-produced, it is still a desirable piece. The technique used by Czech factories involved hand-pressing soda glass into moulds, which kept the quality high despite the large number of items produced.
8in (20.5cm) high, **B**

Better

This vase, designed by Jan Gabrhel for Chlum u Trebone in 1962, was made by blowing glass into a ribbed mould. The colour variation, created by heating the glass for different periods of time, shows a higher level of skill than the process which uses flat colour. Variated glass was a company speciality, but the blue colour in this piece is unusual.
4.5in (11.5cm) high, **D**

Best

Produced in a limited quantity
of around one hundred examples,
this piece was designed for the
Czech Pavilion at the 1958 World's
Fair in Brussels. Its abstract design
is typical of the style outlawed at the
time in other art forms. The quality
and rarity of this piece, made using
techniques that reverse traditional
modes of cutting and casing, are
what make it so desirable.
12.75in (32.4cm) high, **M**

*This unique Jiri Harcuba hand-cut vase
was a gift from the designer to Ronald
Stennett-Willson (see page 139), who was
head of the glass department of the Royal
College of Art in London in the mid-
1960s, when Harcuba also taught there.*

*Although the "Town" pattern is well
known, with an example in Prague's
Decorative Arts Museum, this is the
only known vessel featuring this design.*

*The image is a stylized town plan,
resembling the forms of contemporary
art. The decoration employs a complex
combination of cutting techniques.*

*A Jiri Harcuba hand cut glass pillow
shaped vase. 1965. 8.25in (21cm) high.* **U**

Jirí Harcuba (b. 1928) is known for his unusual cut and engraved
colourless glass objects, which typically feature stylized and expressive
motifs. He served an apprenticeship at the Harrachov glassworks
from 1942 to 1945, before going on to study at the Nový Bor glass
school, where he also later worked. He lectured at the Academy of
Applied Art in Prague in the 1960s and 1970s and was a Visiting
Professor at the Royal College of Art in London from 1965 to 1966.
He became an independent glass artist in 1971.

Britain

British glass design started to become more modern in the 1920s and the 1930s. Away from mass-produced, pressed-glass forms, it was cut glass that reflected this new movement most strongly. Traditional factories based in and around Stourbridge in the West Midlands, the heart of the glassmaking industry in Britain, were at the forefront of this revolution, employing progressive designers to produce work that focused on simple geometric cuts or stylized natural patterns. These designers included Keith Murray (1892–1981) at Stevens & Williams, Clyne Farquharson (1906–72) at Walsh Walsh, and Ludwig Kny (1869–1937) at Stuart. In terms of blown and coloured glass, notable designs are those produced by William Wilson (1905–72) and Barnaby Powell (1891–1939) at Powell & Sons (Whitefriars), and by Paul Ysart (1904–91) at Scotland's Moncrieff Glassworks.

Many of these innovative designs and styles continued to be made after the war, when a new generation of cut-glass designers rose to prominence, including Irene Stevens (b. 1917) who joined Webb Corbett in 1946, David Hammond (b. 1931) who was hired by Thomas Webb the following year, and John Luxton (b. 1920) who joined Stuart in 1949. Appealing and modern as they were, their designs met with limited success from a public that still largely had conservative and staid tastes, and preferred traditionally cut, colourless glass.

In the 1950s, imports of modern Scandinavian coloured glass increased to meet demand from a predominately young or avant-garde audience. A handful of British designers were influenced by this growing success, some of whom worked for existing companies, while others founded or co-founded new factories to produce this type of glass. Rather than simply copy Scandinavian designs, these designers identified key elements of the style and combined them to create something new, with an added British twist.

The most important of these designers was Geoffrey Baxter (1922–95), who joined Whitefriars in 1954 after graduating from the Royal College of Art in London. His first designs were strongly Scandinavian in style, with curving, organic forms in cool greens, blues and greys. His landmark "Textured" range was released in 1967 and, although quite different from his earlier ranges, was again inspired by Scandinavian glass of that decade. Produced in vibrant colours, the range comprised unusual, primarily geometric forms with textured surfaces.

Ronald Stennett-Willson (1915–2009, see page 139) also used strong colours on simple forms. Apart from founding his own factory, King's Lynn Glass, he is notable for his range of candleholders, as well as for his later unique studio glass works. His protégé Frank Thrower (1932–87) co-founded Dartington Glass in 1967, and produced more than 700 commercially successful designs for the company. Many were textured pieces with stylized motifs, or focused on clarity of line, particularly after the company's acquisition by Wedgwood in 1982.

Another key designer was Irish-born Domhnall Ó Broin (1934–2005), who co-founded Caithness Glass in 1961 in northern Scotland. Based on geometric shapes such as the cylinder, forms were unembellished and relied on the clarity of their lines and the material for their success. Colours ranged from austere greys to resonant blues, pinky-purples, and greens inspired by the Scottish landscape.

Left: A 1960s Thomas Webb large "Flair" vase, designed by David Hammond and Stan Eveson in 1961, with yellow rim and amber base with internal air bubbles. The vessels in this scarce, avant-garde range were swung into form after being pierced with a metal spike and a wet stick. 13in (33cm) high, **C**

Centre: A 1970s Dartington Glass midnight grey large "FT58" vase, with moulded, textured Greek key design, designed by Frank Thrower in 1967. Made in four colours and two sizes, this was one of Thrower's most popular forms. 9.5in (24.5cm) high, **B**

Right: A Whitefriars Meadow Green "Banjo" vase, no.9681, from the "Textured" range designed by Geoffrey Baxter in 1967. The form, colours, size, and level of texture indicate value. This is a scarce, desirable colour on a hallmark form. 12.5in (32cm) high, **L**

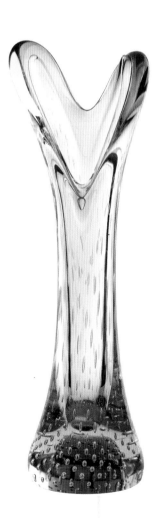

Britain

From the 1960s onwards, the success of British coloured glass inspired by Scandinavian styles saw the start of a steady decline in the popularity of traditional cut glass. Among the companies that shared in the success of this new, modern style were Chance Glass, best known for its handkerchief bowls, which echoed Fulvio Bianconi's "Fazzoletto" (handkerchief) vase for Venini, and United Glass, who produced tableware decorated with printed designs by the prolific Alexander Hardie-Williamson (1907–94). The studio glass movement also began in the 1960s, and would have profound effects on the way glass was made and perceived. One early commercial success was Mdina Glass, founded on Malta by Royal College of Art graduate Michael Harris (1933–94).

Four of a set of six Stevens & Williams for J. Wuidart & Co. "Harlequin" goblets, designed by Ronald Stennett-Wilson in 1953. The vibrant, non-matching colours of this set were considered avant-garde at the time. Each 3.5in (9cm) high, **B** (set)

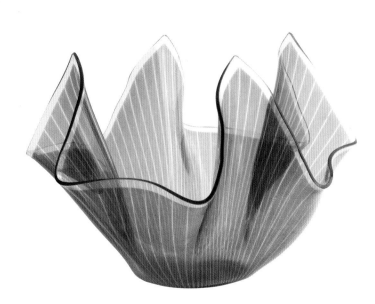

A Stuart barrel vase, cut with alternating vertical lines and columns of lenses, designed by John Luxton, c.1950. This is typical of the more modern designs released by established British cut-glass companies after the war. 7.5in (19cm) high, **G**

A Whitefriars Old Gold "Studio" vase, designed by Peter Wheeler in 1969, with opaque white glass cased in striped orange and colourless glass. This range was produced in response to the growing studio glass movement. 10.25in (26cm) high, **C**

A 1960s–70s Chance Glass purple silkscreen-printed "Cordon" pattern large handkerchief vase. Probably inspired by Venini's fazzoletto bowl, these bowls were produced in many sizes, colours, and patterns. 7in (18cm) high, **A**

A Whitefriars Kingfisher blue "Drunken Bricklayer" vase, no.9673, from the "Textured" range designed by Geoffrey Baxter in 1966.The form was inspired by a pile of bricks. This colour was produced from 1969 to 1974. 8.25in (21cm) high, **L**

A Dartington "Nipple" hexagonal vase, designed by Frank Thrower in 1969. The design, which made waves at the time, is based on the form of the human nipple. Actually a cased orange, this "Flame red" is the rarest colourway. 4.25in (11cm) high, **C**

Ronald Stennett-Willson

Each component is a separate piece of glass, meaning the largest example shown here is made up of 21 pieces.

"Sheringham" candleholders were produced in sizes from one to nine "discs". Larger examples were considerably more expensive at the time and so are harder to find today.

Great skill and experience are required to make all the pieces a consistent size and shape, and to join them together in a straight line.

The "Sheringham" won a Queen's Award for Design in 1967.

They were made in dark blue, colourless, amethyst, topaz, and dark green.

*A group of five late 1960s or 1970s King's Lynn Glass or Wedgwood Glass "Sheringham" candleholders, no.RSW58, designed by Ronald Stennett-Willson in 1967. Tallest 14in (36cm) high, from **B–L** depending on size and colour*

Ronald Stennett-Willson (1915–2009) began his career in glass in 1935 when he started working at glass importers Rydbeck & Norstrom in London. In 1951, he joined J. Wuidart & Co., who specialized in importing Scandinavian glass, and went on to become the company's managing director. He also began designing glass, which was produced in Scandinavian and British factories. In 1960 he opened a shop in London selling Scandinavian design, and later became Reader in Glass at the Royal College of Art, London. He founded his own factory in King's Lynn in 1967 so that he could manufacture his own designs. They proved popular, and the successful company was acquired by Wedgwood in 1969.

Europe

Western European glass was heavily influenced by the powerhouses of Scandinavia and Murano. Forms were either organic, curving, and asymmetric or austerely modern, and were typically executed in vibrant or very cool colours. Cut and pressed glass tended to focus on the optical properties of the form and any patterns applied to the exterior. Founded in the Netherlands in 1878, Leerdam comprised two companies under one brand. In Germany, which was divided after the war, Soviet-controlled Eastern factories vied with the West for design innovation and market share. In West Germany, WMF, founded in 1853 and best known for its metalware, widened the art glass range it had first introduced in 1925.

An East German purple vase with spikey internal indentations, from Lauscha. Glass is typically finely blown. The indentations have been made by pushing a metal rod into the sides. 6in (12.5cm) high, **A**

A 1950s French Cristallerie Schneider "Cordée" vase, with a graduated purple body cased in colourless glass and pulled into "wings". Possibly designed by Charles Schneider (b. 1916), this organic form is typical of the new factory's 1950s designs. 7.5in (19cm) high, **F**

A 1960s East German Vereinigte Lausitzer Glaswerke light blue pressed glass "Lyon" vase. VLG was incorporated into a larger group of companies following World War II. This vase is also produced in smokey grey and light green. 8in (20.5cm) high, **A**

A 1970s East German Schott-Zwiesel "Florida" range vase, designed by Heinrich Löffelhardt. This popular design, with internal bubbles and colourless casing, was made in blue, green, or brown, and in many shapes. 10.25in (26cm) high, **C**

A 1950s East German Vereinigte Lausitzer Glaswerke grey-blue ovoid vase, by Bauhaus designer Wilhelm Wagenfeld, with oval cut lenses by Erich Jachmann. Wagenfeld was VLG's art director from 1935 to 1947; Jachmann later worked for WMF. 6.25in (16cm) high, **D**

A German WMF "Ikora Kristall" vase, with applied graduated red-orange and opaque white powdered enamel with a craquelure effect, cased in colourless glass. Designed by Karl Wiedmann in 1921, the popular "Ikora" range was produced into the 1950s. 9.5in (25cm) high, **C**

A Dutch Leerdam "Unica" glass vase, model AM2059, designed by Floris Meydam in 1956. Meydam joined Leerdam in 1935 and produced many designs for the "Unica" and "Serica" ranges from the 1950s onwards. 5.7in (14.5cm) high, **D**

A 1960s Belgian Val Saint Lambert asymmetric bowl, the pink core cased in colourless glass, with factory gilt label. Freelance designers such as Nanny Still were employed by the factory in the 1960s and 1970s. 13.5in (34cm) long, **C**

A West German Ichendorf mould-blown lead crystal vase by Bleikristall, a company best known for bubbled glass. This design was also produced with a coloured core. 6.5in (16.5cm) high, **A**

A Dutch Leerdam Glasfabriek "Ligne Libre" colourless and turquoise bottle vase, designed by Floris Meydam in 1967. Meydam (b. 1919) was chief designer from 1949 until the 1980s. 15in (41cm) high, **E**

North America

Although inspired by developments in Scandinavia and on Murano, American Mid-Century Modern glass pursued its own path. Extravagant forms and large bottles in fashionable colours were typical, although clean-lined modern tableware was also made. Many notable makers of the period were based in West Virginia, and include Blenko, Viking, Pilgrim, Rainbow, and Bischoff. Of these companies, Blenko was the most successful and influential. Founded in 1922, the company was known for hand-blown glass in bright colours based on stained glass. Its key designers were Winslow Anderson (1917–2007) from 1947 to 1953, Wayne Husted (b. 1927) from 1953 to 1963, and Joel Philip Myers (b. 1934) from 1963 to 1970.

A Blenko "Persian Blue" crackle glass tall stoppered bottle, no. 6029, designed by Wayne Husted in 1959. Although this form was produced until 1964, it was made in this colour in 1959 only. 28.75in (73cm) high, **E**

A Rainbow Art Glass Co. mould-blown turquoise vase, with undulating ribs. Founded in 1942, Rainbow became a subsidiary of Viking Glass in the early 1970s. This form was inspired by Scandinavian glass designs. 10.25in (25.5cm) high, **D**

A Viking Glass mould-blown purple large stoppered bottle, with colourless stopper. In 1944, the New Martinsville Glass Co. was renamed Viking Glass Company. The firm, known for large bottles such as this one, closed in 1986. 26in (66cm) high, **D**

Three 1960s Viking Glass amber glass mushrooms. Pieces such as these were influenced by Scandinavian designs that were inspired by nature. Largest 5.5in (14cm) wide, from **A–B** each

A Morgantown teal mould-blown "Susquehanna" candle vase, no.9960. Morgantown tended to produce thinly blown glass. This angular design has a solid base for stability. 5.5in (14cm) high, **A**

A Morgantown yellow mould-blown bottle vase. Like the blue vase to the left, this vase was inspired by Scandinavian glass. 17in (44cm) high, **C**

A 1960s–70s Pilgrim Glass mould-blown stoppered bottle. Pilgrim was founded in 1949 and its chief designer was Robert Moretti. The company is best known for its "Cranberry" glass, introduced in 1968, and coloured crackle glass. 9.5in (24cm) high, **B**

A Bischoff red bottle with clear stopper, c.1960. Best known for its crackle glass and light fittings, Bischoff was founded in 1922 and closed in 1984. Many designs are similar to, and often mistaken for, those produced by Blenko. 1.5in (34cm) high, **D**

A Blenko graduated red to yellow textured glass vase, designed by Wayne Husted in 1962. Sometimes known as "Amberina", the graduated colours are achieved by reheating areas of the glass after it has been made. 11.5in (29cm) high, **B**

Ceramics

North America

The Mid-Century Modern movement in ceramic design has its roots in the late Art Deco period in North America. There were two distinct branches of North American ceramics at this time: the mass-produced services made by such companies as Red Wing Potteries in Minnesota, Steubenville in Ohio, and the Blue Mountain Pottery in Ontario, and the important field of art ceramics.

In 1937 industrial designer Russel Wright (1904–76) created the "American Modern" service for Steubenville, which is the most widely sold American ceramic dinnerware in history. Wright turned his back on the geometric Art Deco style and took his inspiration from fluid and organic forms instead. Equally revolutionary was his "mix and match" idea of the buyer being able to chose from a palette of complementary colours. His simple, practical, affordable, and accessible wares did much to bring Modernism into American homes in the 1940s and 1950s.

One of the most important catalysts for this new approach to design was a competition held by the Metropolitan Museum of Modern Art in New York in 1940, entitled Organic Design in Home Furnishings. In his competition brief, the head of the museum's department of industrial design, Eliot Noyes, issued a challenge to designers: "In the field of home furnishings there have been no outstanding design developments in recent years. A new way of living is developing, however, and this requires a fresh approach to the design problems."

One of the designers inspired by Noyes's words was Eva Zeisel (1906–2011). In 1942, she designed the all-white "Museum" range for Castleton China, which laid claim to being the first translucent china dinnerware produced in the USA. Although the range was reminiscent of German porcelains exported at the time, the design was entirely original, elegant, and less geometric. Decorative patterns were added around 1949. Zeisel also designed the "Town and Country" range for Red

Top: Frank Irwin, who designed this Metlox "Freeform" dish with the "California Mobile" pattern in 1954, was influenced by contemporary sculptors such as Alexander Calder and Henry Moore. 12.5in (32cm) long, **B**

Bottom: Designed in 1937, the fluid and organic forms of Russel Wright's "American Modern" service hark back to Art Nouveau styles, but with a modern twist. 7in (18cm) long, **A**

Wing in 1947. Other mould-breaking shapes were produced by Metlox Potteries, including the "Free Form" range designed by Frank Irwin (1922–2002).

Many influential ceramicists relocated from Europe to the United States between the wars, and went on to develop highly influential styles. Austrians Otto (1908–2007) and Gertrud Natzler (1908–71) established a studio in Los Angeles in 1938. Gertrud threw the clay and crafted it into perfectly proportioned, simple forms, while Otto experimented with different glazing techniques. He discovered rich, luminous glazes, many of them inspired by Chinese glazes, which also served as inspiration for two other ceramicist couples, Otto (1915–2009) and Vivika Heino (1910–95) in New England and Gordon (b. 1924) and Jane Martz (1929–2007) in Indiana.

As in France, ceramic design in the US was strongly influenced by the work of fine artists who also created art ceramics, such as Henry Varnum Poor (1887–1970). Poor, who had studied painting in London and Paris, used his ceramics as a canvas for his increasingly nonconformist art.

Left: Eva Zeisel brought simplicity and elegance to a distinctly modern shape in her "Museum" range, which she designed in 1942–3. 9.75in (25cm) high. **E**

Right: Now regarded as iconic, the Red Wing "Smart Set" pattern was only produced from 1955 until 1957. 10in (25cm) diam. **A**

Europe

Left: Sleek, elegant, and icy, Gunnar Nylund's tall matt blue glaze vase was designed in the mid 1950s. 13in (33cm) high. **C**

Centre: This 1950s Lenci pottery jug has an exaggerated angular form. The company's wares are typically in the bright palette of provincial northern Italy, while the modelling shows a Germanic influence. 11.75in (30cm) high, **E**

Right: The German firm Rosenthal produced ceramics with simple, organic lines and streamlined forms, as with this 1950s coffee-pot designed by Raymond Loewy. 11in (28cm), **B**

World War II ended in 1945 but its aftereffects were felt well into the 1950s. Wartime frugality persisted and ceramic designers across Europe were still influenced by the Rational style, although there was a glimmer of interest in something more quirky and colourful.

In Scandinavia, a large number of manufacturers produced a wide variety of wares, from the simple streamlined shapes and muted colours used by Gunnar Nylund (1904–97) for the Danish Nymöelle factory to the hand-painted floral faience designs favoured by Johanne Gerber for the Royal Copenhagen factory. The work of both designers has a thoroughly Mid-Century Modern feel, with Nylund inspired by the organic approach of "Soft Modernism" and Gerber by re-assessing Sweden's folk tradition. Companies such as Gustavsberg, Rörstrand, and Arabia employed innovative designers such as Kaj Franck (1911–89) and Stig Lindberg (1916–82) to design distinctly original and influential ranges.

In contrast to the cool colours of wares from the North, the ceramic designers of Italy favoured bright, bold colours and had an almost artisan approach. Artists such as Guido Gambone (1909–69) and manufacturers such as Lenci produced wares that were dominated by shape, pattern, and glaze.

German ceramics of this period fall into two distinct groups: the refinement and simplicity of the designs that Raymond Loewy (1893–1986), a French-born American industrial designer, produced for Rosenthal stand in direct contrast to the bizarre and futuristic pitted glazes of the "Fat Lava" wares produced by factories such as Scheurich, Ruscha, and Bay Keramik. In recent years, there has been a resurgence of interest in these textured volcanic glazes, which were created by many German factories in ever more exotic colours and colour combinations. Loewy, who designed products for more than 200 companies,

lived by his own famous "MAYA" principle – the letters stand for "Most Advanced Yet Acceptable". According to Loewy, "The adult public's taste is not necessarily ready to accept the logical solutions to their requirements if the solution implies too vast a departure from what they have been conditioned into accepting as the norm."

In Britain a similarly conservative approach was taken to ceramic design and the new style developed slowly. Roy Midwinter was one of the first to realize that the Staffordshire factories had to introduce a "new look". On a trip to North America in 1952, he was shocked when a senior buyer told him that he would shoot the next man who came all the way over from Stoke to show him English roses. After appointing Jessie Tait (1928–2010), Hugh Casson (1910–99), and Terence Conran (b. 1931) as designers, Midwinter began producing

wares that fed the new-found optimism of young home-makers. The company's new designs were completely different to anything the Staffordshire potteries had produced before the war.

Left: Designed in 1960, the Midwinter "Cannes" pattern was a reworking of the "Riviera" pattern designed in 1954 by Hugh Casson. The idea of bringing the sun-soaked South of France into their homes was very appealing to buyers, as were innovative shapes such as this celery vase. 6.75in (17cm), **E**

Right: This "Gaiety" slipware jardinière was designed by John Clappison in 1963 for the Hornsea Pottery, which produced some of the most innovative British ceramic wares. 10in (25.5cm) wide, **B**

Scandinavia

The Stockholm Exhibition of 1930 highlighted the extent to which Scandinavian ceramicists had embraced the ideals of the Bauhaus: in the period between the two world wars, they had subdued the flippancy of some Art Deco porcelain with more discreet shapes and decoration, and added rounded shapes and a relaxed elegance to the stern austerity of Functionalism. The "Soft Modernism" of Scandinavian furniture design was also evident, as the simple shapes and "cold" colours that had characterized Scandinavian ceramics for decades were transformed into rippling surfaces and asymmetrical forms.

Mid-century Scandinavian ceramics can be divided into two distinct areas: factory production and art pottery. The Gustavsberg porcelain factory in Sweden was at the forefront of the new movement under the direction of Wilhelm Kåge (1889–1960) and his protégé Stig Lindberg (1916–82). Gunnar Nylund (1904–97) had worked for Nymolle in Denmark, but he is best known for the matt-glazed stoneware he designed for Rörstrand in Sweden. Another Swedish company, Upsala-Ekeby, produced more affordable wares. Under the direction of Vicke Lindstrand (1904–83) from 1942 until 1962, the factory made some good quality, simple organic shapes and designs.

In the 1940s, Kaj Franck (1911–89) produced the aesthetically and financially lean "Kilta" service for Arabia in Finland. Initially a result of the austerities of war, this economy of style became a hallmark of Scandinavian design. The democratisation of society led to a belief that everyone should have an the opportunity to acquire beautiful, functional objects, which in turn produced a definitive Scandinavian style, characterized by simple ease and natural elegance.

A Swedish Upsala-Ekeby footed spherical vase, with tapered neck, decorated with bands of stylized leaf and linear patterns in grey and white. 13in 33cm) high, **C**

Bjørn Wiinblad

A 1950s Danish Nymølle plaque for July. 6in (15cm) diam, **A**

A Swedish Rorstrand ribbed or disced candleholder, the exterior glazed in red, the interior in yellow. 6.75in (17.5cm) high, **B**

A Rörstrand Ateljé (Studio) bowl, c. 1965, with moulded textured decoration and painted marks to the base. 5in (13cm) high, **B**

Two Danish studio earthenware candelabra. 1972. Tallest 15.75in (40cm) high, **H**

Bjørn Wiinblad (1918–2006) was a Danish artist who applied his characteristic style to ceramics, silver, bronze, textiles, and graphics. Wiinblad's lively work was inspired by his love of literature and music, be it grand opera or folk songs. His pieces feature whimsical round-faced figures in period costume, often surrounded by natural elements – twining vines, floral wreaths, and fantastical trees. Wiinblad was an important designer for the Rosenthal porcelain company in Bavaria, but it was his collaboration with Nymølle in Denmark (a company he went on to own) that brought his work to a wider audience.

Royal Copenhagen

Post-war optimism presented a great opportunity for Royal Copenhagen, founded in Denmark in 1775, to encourage its designers to embrace a definitive style characterized by aesthetic simplicity, natural elegance, and perfect craftsmanship. This style was adopted with great flair in stoneware and porcelain.

With its sober grey glaze and simple blue line around the rim, the "Blue Line" faience dinner service designed by architect Grethe Meyer (1918–2008) in 1965 became the most popular Danish service of the second half of the 20th century. Anne-Marie Trolle (b. 1944) worked at the factory from 1966 until 1972, and her designs included "Domino", a refined porcelain dinner service that won numerous awards. Gertrud Vasegaard (1913–2007), previously an independent potter, designed dinnerwares with an Oriental influence for Royal Copenhagen from 1959 until 1975, while other renowned artists and designers working for the company during this period included Axel Salto (1889–1961), Thorkild Olsen (1890–1973), Magnus Stephensen (1903–84), and Erik Magnussen (b. 1940).

The output of the Alumina factory that made earthenware for Royal Copenhagen was dominated by the designs of Nils Thorsson (1898–1975). His "Marselis" range of affordable, functional wares was decorated sparingly with ribs and geometric patterns picked out on solid glazes in natural tones. The vases he designed in the 1960s and 1970s were among Royal Copenhagen's most popular ranges.

Bing and Grondahl, established in 1853, used many of the same artists and ceramicists as Royal Copenhagen. The sculptor and silversmith Henning Koppel (1918–81) designed a mould-breaking service for the company in the early 1960s. While simple and functional, its generous, organic shapes in gloss-white porcelain evoked extravagance. An icon of its time, the service became known as "White Koppel". Royal Copenhagen bought Bing and Grøndahl in 1987.

A 1950s Royal Copenhagen Fayance vase, no.182/3101, designed by Inge Lise Sorensen and Marianne Johnson. 14.5in (37cm) high, **D**

A 1950s Royal Copenhagen Fayance vase by Inge-Lise Sorensen and Marianne Johnson. This is known as the "Surreal" series, due to its unusual motifs. 7in (18cm) high, **C**

A large 1970s Royal Copenhagen "Fajance" vase by Nils Thorsson. 7.5in (19cm) high, **B**

A Royal Copenhagen "Tenera" vase designed by Grethe Helland-Hansen c.1969–74. 7.5in (19cm) high, **C**

A 1970s Royal Copenhagen vase by Ellen Malmer, with brown abstract design. 6.5in (17cm) high, **C**

Stig Lindberg

(1916-82)

Stig Lindberg (1916–82) studied painting at the University College of Arts, Crafts and Design in Stockholm. In 1937 he joined the Swedish pottery Gustavsberg, where he worked under art director Wilhelm Kåge. Lindberg was made chief designer in 1949, and went on to design a huge range of pieces, including mass-produced wares and one-off masterpieces, for Gustavsberg before leaving the company in 1980.

Although his output was extremely diverse, ranging from wall plaques to folk-inspired figurines, Lindberg is best known for his hand-painted plates and dishes, in particular those featuring leaf shapes. His bold forms and asymmetrical shapes were sparingly decorated with motifs inspired by traditional folk patterns or nature. With its sculptural, elliptical forms and fluid, whimsical designs, the "Faience" range had a simple, organic elegance previously unseen in Scandinavian ceramics and proved to be great success for the firm. With its combinations of ochre, blue, green, and red with black accents, the range's colour scheme was typical of post-war colour palettes.

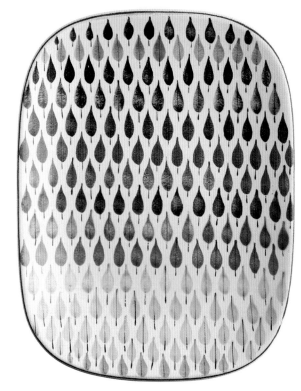

A Gustavsberg platter designed by Stig Lindberg c.1940–50. 12.5in (31.5cm) wide, **F**

A Stig Lindberg studio ceramic bowl dating from c.1950. 9.5in (24cm) wide, **E**

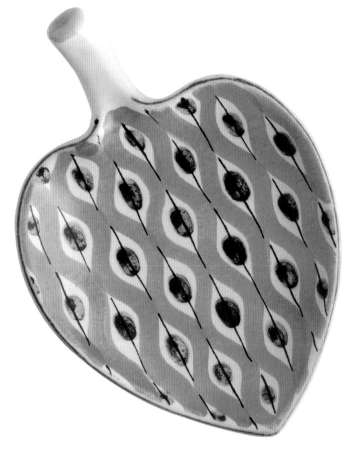

A 1950s Swedish Gustavsberg small leaf tray by Stig Lindberg, with green decoration. 4.75in (12cm) long, **B**

A melon-shaped Gustavsberg vase
designed by Stig Lindberg c.1940–50,
with pink stripes and scalloped collar.
8.5in (21.5cm) high, **G**

Finland
Denmark
Sweden

Many smaller Scandinavian ceramic factories produced interesting and influential work in the mid-century period. In Finland, the main company was Arabia, established in 1874 by Swedish manufacturer Rörstrand. After the war a team of new artists, including Kaj Franck (1911–89) and Ulla Procopé (1921–68), joined the company.

In Denmark, Saxbo was established in 1929 by Nathalie Krebs (1895–1978) and Gunnar Nylund (1904–97), who left in 1930 to join Röstrand. Eva Stæhr-Nielsen (1911–76) joined Saxbo in 1932, and she and Krebs produced matt-glazed stoneware in simple bold forms with Chinese-inspired glazes.

Founded in 1947 by Per and Annelise Linnemann-Schmidt, Palshus produced classical forms, devoid of decoration, with stunning glazes. Another Danish company, Nymolle was founded in 1936 to produce inexpensive ceramics, mirroring ranges by other companies. There were also a number of successful studio potters working in Denmark at this time and, in Sweden, in addition to the three main companies (Gustavsburg, Rörstrand and Upsala-Ekeby), there were also many small companies producing studio ceramics

An Arabia porcelain matt-glazed teapot by Ulla Procopé, c.1953. The pot's rounded shape, flattened lid and cane handle show an Asian influence. 6in (15.25cm) high, **A**

A 1950s Arabia oxblood-glazed ginger jar by Francesca Mascitti-Lindhl. The shape and glazes show an Oriental influence. 4in (10cm) high, **A**

A 1960s Nymølle vase designed by Gunnar Nylund. 10.5in (27cm), **D**

A 1950s Danish Palshus teapot by Frode Bahnsen. Utilitarian ware was part of the Scandinavian aesthetic. 8in (20.5cm) high, **C**

A rare 1950s Danish Palshus tapered stoneware vase by Per Linnemann-Schmidt. 9in (23cm) high, **D**

A 1939 Royal Copenhagen stoneware Indian bowl, covered in mottled brown, cream, and blue glaze. 11.5in (29cm) diam. **W**

A 1940s Arne Bang workshop vase, with brown and taupe glaze. 5in (12.5cm) high, **B**

A 1940s Arne Bang green stoneware vase with ribbed (cog) design. 4.5in (11.5cm) high, **B**

Danish ceramic designer Axel Salto (1889–1961) is renowned for his sophisticated use of sumptuous glazes and his experimental, sculptural forms inspired by nature. Salto's ceramics can be categorized according to three main styles: fluted, budding, and sprouting. Pieces from the latter category bring to mind growth and movemement, with the glaze running freely over the richly textured surfaces. Royal Copenhagen produced Salto's designs from the 1930s until his death.

A 1950s Danish Saxbo vase with brown mottled glaze, designed by Edith Sonne Brunn. 8.5in (21.5cm) high, **D**

A 1960s Danish studio chamotte clay stoneware vase by Conny Walther. 7in (8cm) high, **D**

A 1943 gourd-shaped stoneware vase, covered in eggshell semi-matt glaze. 4.25in (11cm) mid diam. **M**

Germany

West Germany's ceramics factories began to re-emerge in the 1950s, once the industry had started to recover after the war and division of the country. Pre-war ideas, many of them born of the Modernist movement and the Bauhaus, were revived and developed, and by the end of the decade ceramics were once again exported in large numbers. Designs tended to be hand-painted on slip-moulded wares, with outlined areas of colour that contrasted with black or off-white backgrounds.

By the early 1960s, this approach was mainly replaced by experimentation with the decorative effects of glazes, which paralleled the work of many ceramicists working in the United States, such as Otto Natzler (1908–2007). The West German potters mostly used drip glazes, with one glaze running over another, usually in a contrasting colour or a different thickness, resulting in a lava-like effect. Many studio potters have worked with glazes that create craters and bubbles in their surface, but no potter or factory has produced the quantity or variety achieved by the West Germans between the late 1950s and the late 1970s, the golden period of so-called "Fat Lava" wares. Many factories made these distinctive wares, with Otto Keramik, Bay Keramic, Dümler & Breiden, Jopeko, and Carstens among the most important.

The 1970s saw a true explosion in experimentation and innovation with pots of all types, from floor vases to miniature bowls, made in bizarre shapes and covered in dazzling colours and patterns.

A Ruscha pitcher, shape no.313, with dripped red glaze, designed by Kurt Tschorner in 1954. This iconic shape was produced in more than 50 different colourways. 6.25in (16cm) high, **C**

A 1970s Roth Keramik vase, with moulded red gloss glazed concave areas between bubble-textured black-glazed strands, 4.5in (11cm) high, **B**

A 1960s–70s Jasba vase, with creamy white glaze and resist pattern of stylized plants, highlighted in green and red. 5in (12.5cm) high, **C**

A 1960s Gräflich Ortenburg jug vase, form no.619, designed by Irene Paskinski, with a light blue volcanic lava glaze over a matt dark grey glaze. 4.75in (12cm) high, **B**

An East German Strehla jug vase, with tube-lined black lava glaze banded and circle design over a blue glaze. 18cm high, **A**

A West German Scheurich tapering vase, with glossy light blue and cream drip effect glaze. 10.25in (26cm) high, **A**

A horse motif has been cut through the grey bubbly "Fat Lava" glaze of this Scheurich floor vase to reveal the red underglaze. 18in (46cm) high, **C**

Founded as a wholesale business for glass and china in 1928, Scheurich started producing ceramic wares in the 1950s, and went on to become West Germany's largest ceramics manufacturer, a position it held until the 1980s. The company produced a wide range of shapes and decorative glazes, and is particularly noted for its floor vases. The main designer from 1955 onwards was Heinz Siery (b. 1927), who had trained in Höhr-Grenzhausen in the Rhineland, a centre of the German ceramic industry. He designed many iconic forms, and is perhaps best known for the tall "271" jug with its distinctive angled handle, which was produced in numerous different glazes. Scheurich always used a white clay and marks are almost exclusively moulded.

France

Some of the most individualistic Mid-Century Modern ceramics were created by titans of modern art: Gaugin, Picasso, Cocteau, and Chagall produced works in ceramic, ranging from decorative yet functional pieces such as plates to spectacular figural sculptures. While functional objects for the home have often been regarded as mere utensils, many designers in the 1950s recognized the potential for bringing a sculptural quality to ceramics that would transcend utility.

The most famous and prolific mid-century artist to produce ceramics was Pablo Picasso (1881–1973), who made thousands of ceramic works throughout his career, many of which were available in limited editions ranging from 25 to 500, making it possible for many more people to "own a Picasso". Picasso's worked closely with Georges and Suzanne Ramie, who ran the Madoura pottery studio in Vallauris, France. He designed and painted plates, jugs, vases, and tiles, as well as creating sculptures in clay.

Like many artist of his generation, Jean Cocteau (1889–1963) experimented with decorating ceramic blanks. Very similar to his graphic work, his ceramics are mostly unadorned and decorated freely, and they have a spontaneity and vitality about them. Cocteau described his work as "tatooing the clay".

During the war, Georges Jouve (1910–64), who had trained as an artist, spent some time in Dieulefit, a potters' village in the south of France. Inspired by the local religious figurines, he started to make ceramics of his own.

A red terracotta charger painted with a female profile by Jean Cocteau, who developed a method of "drawing" directly on to terracotta. 14in (35.5cm) diam, **N**

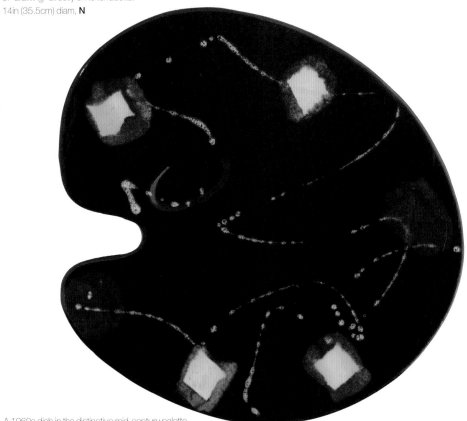

A 1960s dish in the distinctive mid-century palette shape. Such was the mass-production of this period that wares often cannot be assigned to a specific factory. 12in (30.5cm) wide, **B**

With its traditional, simple form and applied plaque, this vase is typical of Georges Jouve's work in the 1950s. The decoration is carved directly on to the body and picked out with glaze. 14in (36cm) high, **W**

"Soleil" vase made by Georges Jouve c.1948. Jouve preferred working with his hands to using a potter's wheel, lending his work and organic, sculptural appearance. 12in (30.5cm) high, **W**

Pablo Picasso

A Picasso vase, numbered 171/200. c1947 8. 14.5in (37cm). A

Pablo Picasso (1881–1973) would often manipulate clay bottles made by Georges and Suzanne Ramie at the Madoura Pottery into fantastical figural shapes such as the one shown here. Decorated with stylized depictions of the body, these designs are reminiscent of his drawn and painted work. This piece is an example of his unique sculptural work – the hand of the master conquering another medium. Picasso's ceramics convey a sense spontaneity, vitality, and vibrancy. He regarded his ceramics as a form of canvas that allowed him to experiment with form and decoration, the personal and the universal.

Italy

Unlike Scandinavia, with its distinctive, recognizable style, Italy produced as many different styles as there were ceramics factories and designers. After the war, the Italian pottery industry saw a rapid cross-pollination of studio, artist, and commercial pottery. This resulted in Italy developing hugely successful mass-produced art pottery with individual quality.

The figural medium in Mid-Century Modern Italian pottery was expressed most successfully by Marcello Fantoni (1915–2011) and Guido Gambone (1909–69). Already well established as a ceramicist before the war, Fantoni continued to consolidate his reputation between the 1950s and the 1970s. He gained an international reputation for his lustrous colours and glazes and stylized motifs. He was known for his large-scale ewers and vases with textured surfaces and strong primary colours. In the 1950s he was commissioned to design large figural sculptures, which, although inspired by Etruscan artefacts, exude the Modern aesthetic. His combined interest in modern art and his Italian heritage led to the creation of new and unique forms that were frequently more sculptural than functional.

The decoration on Gambone's expressive earthenware was also extremely influential, with many smaller Italian factories replicating his style. The decoration mainly consisted of uncomplicated line drawings, abstract figures, and Cubist-inspired patterns.

Good

This bulbous vase by Marcello Fantoni is a pleasing shape, with a good colour combination of a hand-painted red/brown band over a yellow drip glaze, but it lacks the exuberance collectors look for in Fantoni ceramics. Although proficient, it is small and rather uninspiring, and the style is not consistent with Fantoni's work. 7in (17.5cm) high, **D**

Better

The strong red-glazed background, turquoise interior, scrafitto, and painted decoration of stylized gossiping women of this vase, dating from c.1960, are all classic Fantoni. The work of Pablo Picasso, Georges Braque, and Juan Gris was hugely influential with Italian potteries at this period. The only drawback to this piece is its small size. 6.75in (17cm) high, **F**

Guido Gambone

The earthenware vessels designed by Guido Gambone (1909–69) frequently feature simple painted and incised patterns or figures, often animals. While many of Gambone's shapes are modern and he made use of modern techniques, his work was inspired by the simplicity of ancient Etruscan pottery or early Greek ceramics. The colours are often muted, although many of the vessels produced for his "Faenzerella" range have vibrant hues. Some of his vessels are covered with lava glazes

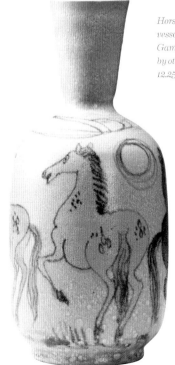

Horses cavorting around a vessel was a motif favoured by Gambone, and much copied by other Italian factories. 12.25in (31cm) high. **L**

Best

The geometric form and angular decoration of this imposing and rare "Satire in Love" sculpture show a clear Cubist influence. The piece iis inspired by the traditional "Harlequin" character of the Italian Commedia dell'Arte of the late 16th century. Its design may also derive from the Italian Futurist movement of the early 20th century. Fantoni's glazes, motif, and colour palette look thoroughly contemporary. 15in (38cm) high, **N**

Italy

Italian ceramics produced by unidentified potteries and designers far outnumber the known works. Designs, colours, and textures are often closely copied from, or inspired by, works by Marcello Fantoni (1915–2011) and Guido Gambone (1909–69), but some pieces are entirely unique.

These wares were produced in large quantities for export to the rest of Europe and the United States, or to be bought as souvenirs by tourists visiting Italy. The majority bear no other mark than "Italy" and a mysterious number, which may indicate the pattern or shape. In the 1950s and 1960s, designers working for factories like Bitossi took their inspiration from the colours of the Mediterranean – vivid blue and greens – and produced stylish new shapes. The surfaces are often decorated with bands of embossed crosses, runes, and symbols.

One of the principal manufacturers was Richard-Ginori in Doccia. The factory was orginially established in 1735, and the 1950s saw a complete change of direction in design. The principal designer was Giovanni Gariboldi (1908–71), who produced tableware with linear, abstract patterns. Gio Ponti (1891–1979) also designed for Ginori, having been the company's artistic director from 1923 until 1930.

This Bitossi "Rimini Blue' vase was designed by Aldo Londi in 1953. The Mediterranean colours are typical of the company, as are the impressed bands of symbols. 8.5in (21.5cm) high, **A**

Redolent of the Art Deco period, this quilted ceramic vessel was designed in the 1950s by Gio Ponti for Richard Ginori. 8.5in (22cm) high, **M**

A 1950s Italian vase inspired by the work of Guido Gambone, decorated with a sgrafitto pattern of a goat's head and leafy sprigs on a textured pink glazed background. 5.75in (14.5cm) high, **A**

A 1950s–60s Italian blue textured jug with hand-painted black lines and multi-coloured ovals. 7in (17.25in) high, **A**

An Italian tapering vase, hand-painted with random multi-coloured textured squares. Vases of this type were vaguely inspired by modern art. 8in (21cm) high, **A**

A 1970s Italian vase with thin neck, with yellow, blue and brown lava-glazed band. These earth colours were also popular in the 1960s. 11in (27.5cm) high, **D**

As new shapes were introduced, hand-painted humorous figures such as this one proved popular and inexpensive decorative elements. 4.5in (15.5cm) high, **B**

Piero Fornasetti

A mid-late 20th century set of 24 Italian Piero Fornasetti "Adam and Eve" pattern porcelain plates. Each 10.25in (26cm) diam. **M** (the set)

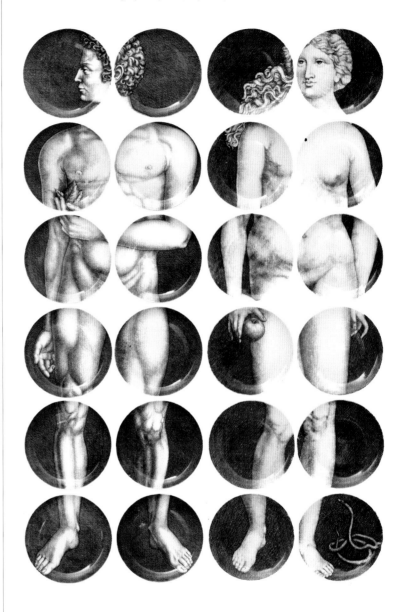

Piero Fornasetti (1913–88) was a prolific designer who drew inspiration from the Classics, the Renaissance, and Surrealist art. His style broke away from that of his contemporaries and was based instead on *trompe l'œil*, illusionism, and architectural perspectives. Fornasetti used a plethora of motifs such as the sun, the moon, time, faces, harlequins, and playing cards. As well as designing furniture (see page 56–57) and interiors, he produced a range of porcelain designs that were generally transfer-printed on to blanks.

Britain

In terms of inspiring British ceramic design, the most influential event of the 1950s was the Festival of Britain. The 1940s had been the age of Utility – plain wares in very few shapes. Held in 1951, the Festival of Britain demonstrated that the principles of modernity could be applied to everything from the exteriors of buildings through to a simple plate. The importance of well-designed homewares to British industry was further emphasized when the state-funded Council of Industrial Design opened the Design Centre in London in 1956.

Throughout the 1950s, Midwinter was the leading company in contemporary tableware. Roy Midwinter had returned from the US with a wealth of new ideas and employed a team of talented designers including Jessie Tait (1928–2010), Hugh Casson (1910–99), and Terence Conran (b. 1931). These designers created colourful and stylish patterns for a new generation, for people who desired modern designs at affordable prices. The main shapes used for these new patterns were the "Stylecraft" and "Fashion" ranges. The launch of the "Stylecraft" range in 1953 was accompanied by a new marketing strategy, designed to encourage new brides to buy. Instead of selling a dinner or tea set, the company produced a 20-piece "starter set", which was to retail at 39 shillings and 9 pence (under £2!).

Founded in 1873, Poole Pottery enjoyed particular success with its Art Deco wares. Robert Jefferson joined the company in the 1950s, and alongside such artisans as Leslie Elsden, Guy Sydenham, and Tony Morris, developed two lines that are probably the most famous of all Poole's output: the "Delphis" and "Aegean" ranges. "Delphis" is easily recognized: it is psychedelic, with vibrant colours and designs inspired by artists such as Mondrian, Warhol, Matisse, and Pollock. "Aegean" is more subtle, with the sgraffito technique used to create the "silhouette" patterns that make this range so distinctive.

One of the most iconic designs of the 1950s is the "Homemaker" range, created by Enid Seeney (1931–2011) for the Ridgway Potteries, Stoke-on Trent. Decorated with black stylized images of household items from tables and chairs to plant pots, the easily affordable transfer-printed range was first sold in Woolworths (for two and a half pence a plate) in 1957, and remained in production until 1970.

Left: Jessie Tait designed the "Zambesi" early morning teapot for Midwinter in 1956. With its organic form and animal print inspiration, it remains one of her most recognizable and imitated designs. 5in (13cm) high, **C**

Right: This "Homemaker" plate, designed by Enid Seeney for Ridgway is perhaps one of the most recognizable objects of the 1950s. The inexpensive range gave homes a fashionable look. Both the simple forms and the highly characteristic motifs sum up the essence of 1950s styling. 10in (25.5cm), **A**

Britain

The design and production of much of the output of British ceramic factories was dictated by the tastes and aspirations of a new generation of young homemakers who sought to turn their backs on the austerity of the war years with modern products and furnishings. Many potteries introduced lines to attract these new buyers, including Rye Pottery in Sussex, and Beswick and H. J. Wood in Staffordshire. As elsewhere in Europe, designers took their inspiration from organic forms, producing curved and biomorphic shapes. These ceramics also reflected the new informal style of living and entertaining.

Carlton Ware strived to be at the forefront of popular trends and sought out designers who could produce innovative, original designs. They created a wide variety of decorative ceramics that captured the mood of the era, such as the "Orbit" range.

Susan Williams-Ellis (1918–2007) started production at the Portmeirion Pottery in Stoke-on-Trent using blanks from another manufacter. Her most famous design was the cylindrical "Totem" range with its distinctive embossed pattern, launched in 1963.

Wedgwood launched a range of tableware by Eric Ravilious (1903–42), which was designed in 1938 but not put into production until after the war. It hence shows no influences from the "New Look" and was not particularly popular with the public at the time.

While most potteries were putting all their energies into mass production, some companies, such as Denby in Derbyshire, introduced handmade and hand-painted lines. Each piece was unique and appealed to customers who wanted something a little different. The "Glynbourne" range by Glyn Colledge (1922–200) was particularly successful.

Troika was established in 1963 in Cornwall. The firm produced wares inspired by the local Cornish landscape and the St Ives group of abstract artists, including Ben Nicholson and Barbara Hepworth.

Designed in the late 1950s by Peter Forster, this Carlton Ware "Orbit" teapot was inspired, in both form and name, by the fascination with space exploration. 6in (15cm) high, **B**

An early Rye Pottery "Cigar" pattern pin dish, thrown by David Sharp in the mid-1950s. 4.25in (10.5cm) diam, **A**

A 1960s Denby "Glynbourne" vase, shape
no. GB870, with hand-painted stylized foliate
decoration, designed by Glyn Colledge.
9in (23cm), **B**

A Denby "Classic" range vase, designed by Kenneth
Clark. This austere range was released in 1960.
9in (23cm) high, **B**

A Wedgwood "1951 Festival of Britain" mug,
designed by Norman Makinson, printed in black
with the festival emblem. 2.75in (7cm) high, **E**

A 1950s H. J. Wood Piazza Ware vase, with bold,
abstract hand-painted decoration and an
asymmetric shape. 9.5in (24cm) high, **A**

Metalware and textiles

Introduction: metalware

Sleek and easily moulded, metal was an ideal material for the modern shapes of the mid-century. Its durability meant that those who worked in metal did so with an awareness of the permanence of their work, creating beautiful pieces ranging from toast racks to cocktail shakers.

Designs were strongly influenced by streamlined pieces from the 1920s and 1930s, but matt finishes were more common than the shiny surfaces that had characterized Art Deco and Modernist design. Decoration was largely kept to a minimum, although textured surfaces were popular in Britain and America, championed by designers such as Gerald Benney (1930–2008) and Paul Evans (1931–87). In Norway Grete Prytz Kittelsen (1917–2010) also broke away from the trend for simplicity with her brightly coloured enamel kitchenware for Catherinholm.

As in other disciplines, Scandinavia took the lead. Silver design was dominated by Denmark's Georg Jensen Company, which boasted designers such as Henning Koppel (1918–81), Bertel Gardberg (1916–2007), and Magnus Stephensen (1903–84).

New production techniques simplified the casting process, making possible the industrial manufacture of a wide range of new silver shapes. Often elegant and organic, these designs became hugely influential across Europe and the rest of the world. A former Jensen designer, Carl Poul Petersen (1895–1977) established his own company in Canada, bringing the Scandinavian aesthetic to North America.

Although many outstanding designs were produced in silver, the fact that many countries were substantially poorer than they had been before the war meant that expensive pieces were less in demand. Silversmiths were also increasingly encouraged to engage in industrial design. The war effort had seen huge advances in the industrial application of aluminium and stainless steel alloys, and these new inexpensive materials were now readily available for use within the decorative arts. Many talented smiths chose to work with aluminium, steel, and chrome, often combining these metals with wood to produce simple, usable objects. Unlike silver, these stylish pieces did not tarnish and so were easier to maintain, making them attractive to consumers.

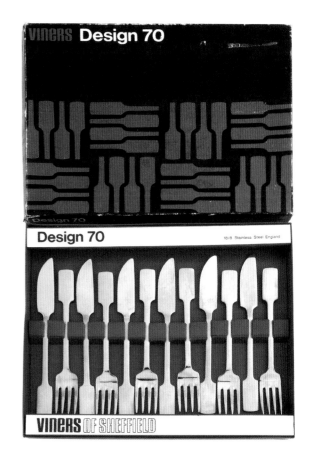

One of the most notable examples of a silversmith turned industrial designer was Royal College of Art graduate Robert Welch (1929–2000), who had visited Sweden in 1954 and been inspired by the stainless steel wares of Sigurd Persson (1914–2003). Welch became design director of Old Hall Tableware in 1955 and designed a range of pieces that not only soon became staples in cafés across Britain but also won him three Design Council Awards and propelled stainless steel and Old Hall to a worlwide audience.

Many other designers also created stylish pieces in base metals, including many other graduates of the Royal College of Art, such as David Mellor (1930–2009). In Scandinavia, Arne Jacobsen (1902–71) designed the "Cylinda-Line" range of stainless steel tableware. In France, Lino Sabattini (b. 1925) designed avant-garde electroplated pieces for Christofle, while in the USA Russel Wright (1904–76) produced streamlined tablewares in aluminium and Tommi Parzinger (1903–81) made brass objects for Dorlyn.

Stainless steel, aluminium, and chrome objects increasingly began to rival silver and pewter for design excellence. These objects were functional, beautiful and, best of all, affordable, meaning that Mid-Century metalware design could be enjoyed by all.

Left: The spindly spout and handle of this watering can designed by Carl Auböck in 1952. 6.25in (16cm) long, **D**

Right: This silver 1960s carafe was designed by Hans Bunde, one of the most important silversmiths working for Danish silverware factory Carl M. Cohr in the 1950s and 1960s. The company also produced stainless steel pieces from 1931 onwards. 9in (23cm) high, **L**

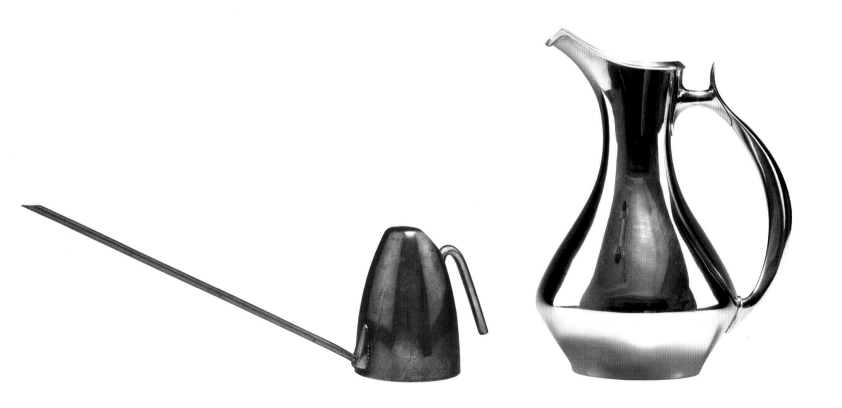

Britain

The Royal College of Art in London was the driving force behind British metalware in the 1950s, 1960s, and 1970s. Designers including Robert Welch (1929–2000), David Mellor (1930–2007), Gerald Benney (1930–2008), and Stuart Devlin (b. 1931) all trained at the RCA under Professor Robert Gooden before founding their own studios and producing innovative new silver, silver plate and gold designs. British smiths were also keen to embrace mass-produced design and many, most notably Robert Welch, turned their expertise to stainless steel. Simple, curving forms are typical of both precious and base metal designs, but unlike the smooth Scandinavian pieces that had inspired them, many British designs featured textured, bark-like surfaces.

Introduced in 1962, Robert Welch's "Alveston" tableware was Old Hall's flagship range in the 1960s. As well as the cutlery shown here, it includes a teapot shaped like a modern Aladdin's lamp. 6in (15cm) long, **A**

With their futuristic shapes, these 1960s stainless steel salt and pepper shakers by Viner's of Sheffield seem to evoke spaceships. 4in (10cm) high. **A**

This jug features the logo designed by Abram Games for the 1951 Festival of Britain. 5in (12.5cm) high, **A**

Designed in 1958, David Mellor's "Pride" silver tea service won a Design Council Award in 1959 for both its aesthetic and practical qualities. 69oz (1.96 kg) approx, **L**

Leslie Durbin was a pupil of silversmith Omar Ramsden and purchased his pattern books after Ramsden's death. The feet on this 1954 silver chocolate pot by Durbin are from a Ramsden design. 12in (31cm) high, 36oz (1.02 kg) approx, **J**

The "Conrah" range was designed by Ronald Hughes in 1967. Made in Wales of aluminium, pieces such as this vase were anodized to give them colour and then cut with patterns. 10in (25.5cm) high, **B**

These striking Old Hall candlesticks show Robert Welch's commitment to the Scandinavian philosophy of designing functional, beautiful, and affordable everyday objects. 9in (23cm) high, **B**

Stuart Devlin

(b. 1931)

Top: In the early 1970s Devlin created a range of stainless steel tableware for Viner's of Sheffield. Each piece featured a textured gold-plated area. 5.25in (13.5cm) high, **B**

Centre: Devlin is known for creating novelty forms, including "surprise" eggs and desk ornaments, such as this pensive toad from 1973. 1.25in (3cm) high, 3oz (85g) approx, **F**

Bottom left: In 1974 Devlin engaged craftsman Brian Martin to produce his furniture designs. This "Filigree" loveseat is believed to be a one-off. 31in (79cm) long, **O**

Bottom right: This 1973 jug is unusual, as the silver is hammered rather than shiny and smooth. The texture still contrasts with the gold-coloured detail on the inside of the handle. 11.25in (28.5cm) high, **M**

Opposite: Shown with four candleholders, this 1969 candelabra seems to be influenced by dandelion puffs and a 1960s idea of space travel pods. It features Devlin's characteristic use of surface contrast. **Q**

In 1957, Stuart Devlin began to study for a Diploma of Arts in gold and silversmithing at Melbourne College, Australia. The course should have taken three years full-time, but Devlin not only completed it in one year, he did it part-time and achieved the highest marks ever awarded. As a result he won three travelling scholarships, one of which he spent at the Royal College of Art in London, where he studied under Professor Robert Gooden.

In an unprecedented move, the Worshipful Company of Goldsmiths purchased a large number of the pieces Devlin made at college and gave him a major commission before he had graduated. In 1962, Devlin returned to Australia, where he won a competition to design the country's first decimal coinage. He moved permanently to England in 1965. In 1982 he was granted the Royal Warrant.

Over the course of his career, Devlin has designed furniture, interiors, jewellery, and stainless steel objects, but he remains best known for his silverware, which often features contrasts between shiny silver surfaces and textured gold. He set out to create work that is true to his four maxims: "That the future is much more important than the past, that creativity is paramount, that skill is fundamental, and that the justification for being a goldsmith is to enrich the way people live and work."

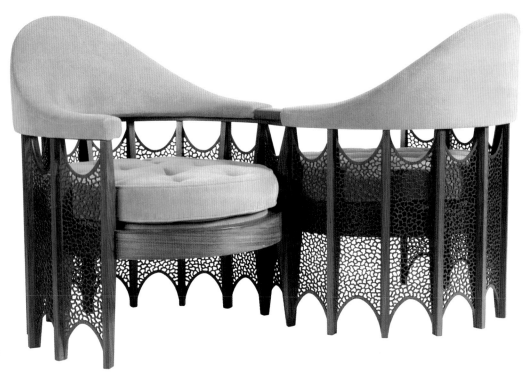

Scandinavia

Scandinavia dominated metalware design in the 1950s, 1960s, and 1970s. Perhaps the most outstanding silverware was designed by Henning Koppel (see "A Closer Look") for the Danish firm Georg Jensen, but Tapio Wirkkala (1915–85) also created several strikingly elegant, organic forms, which were manufactured by Kultakeskus in Finland. Other Jensen designers, such as Sigvard Bernadotte (1907–2002) and Jørgen Jensen (1895–1966), helped put the company at the forefront of silver design. Bernardotte's designs are typically geometric and streamlined, while Jørgen Jensen's are sleek.

Another top designer who worked for Georg Jensen was Arne Jacobsen (1902–71). As well as silver designs, he created a range of stainless steel wares for Stelton and a range of stainless steel cutlery (manufactured by Jensen) so futuristic that it was featured in Stanley Kubrick's film *2001: A Space Odyssey*. Several Scandinavian designers, including Grete Prytz (1917–2010) and Herbert Krenchel (b. 1922), embraced enamelling. Krenchel's enamelled "Krenit" bowls are today regarded as a benchmark of household design.

This sleek 1950s silver sugar shaker by Frantz Hingelberg for Aarhus features Bakelite accents. Many mid-century smiths combined metal with other materials to create functional objects. 5.25 in (13.5cm) high, **F**

Dating from c.1965, this Danish stainless steel teapot is similar in form to the "Alveston" teapot designed by Robert Welch for Old Hall in 1962. 5in (13cm) high, **A**

Designed in 1954, Herbert Krenchel's "Krenit" bowls were machine-pressed from plates of thin steel. The use of colour makes them unusual for metalware of this period. Largest 6.25in (16cm) diam, **C** each

All the pieces in Arne Jacobsen's "Cylinda-Line", including this cocktail shaker, are based on simple, stainless steel unadorned cylindrical forms.
9in (23cm) high, **B**

The hammered surface of this early 1970s Tapio Wirkkala silver jug is reminiscent of the textured surfaces of many of his glass designs. Both suggest the surface of blocks of ice. 10in (25cm) high, 27oz (768.5g), **L**

Henning Koppel

Koppel did not always give his designs elegant names. The precursor to this pitcher, no.992, was called the "Pregnant Duck".

This design was inspired by another highly modern Georg Jensen pitcher: the 432F, designed by Johan Rohde.

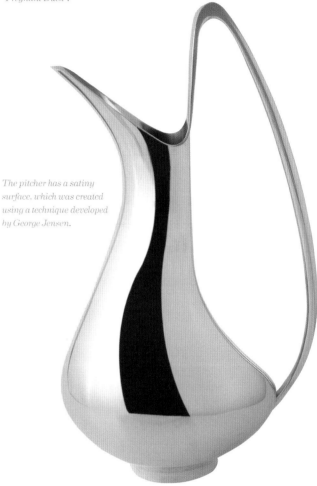

The pitcher has a satiny surface, which was created using a technique developed by George Jensen.

A 1950s Georg Jensen water pitcher, designed by Henning Koppel, no. 1052. 16.5in (42cm) high, **U**

Henning Koppel (1918–81) considered himself an "anti-functionalist", utterly opposed to the dominant idea of the time that form should follow function. The silverware he designed for the Georg Jensen firm from 1946 onwards was fluid, sinuous, and beautiful before it was functional. It was also very different to the wares that had traditionally been made at Jensen, apart from those by Johan Rohde. Although apparently simple, many of these pieces were extremely difficult to produce, pushing both craftsman and the material itself to their limits. Koppel's designs for Jensen ranged from large sculptural bowls to jewellery. His water pitchers, including the "Swan" pitcher, are widely considered to be his best work.

North America

Notable metalware was produced by polymath designers in America. Russel Wright (1904–76), famous for his ceramics, produced a range of streamlined tablewares in aluminium, while Tommi Parzinger (1903–81), better known for his furniture, designed large, polished-brass pieces for Dorlyn. Paul Evans (1931–87), who notably created large metal furniture, also produced some strikingly simple domestic items. In Mexico, American-born silversmith William Spratling (1900–67) began to use wooden handles for his silverware, following the trend set by Mid-Century metalware in other countries. In Canada, Carl Poul Petersen (see "A Closer Look"), who had trained under Georg Jensen, helped introduce Scandinavian style to a new North American audience.

These Carl Poul Petersen miniature tazzas (footed bowls) dating from c.1950 can be used as candlesticks when reversed. 3.75in (9.5cm) diam, **G**

Paul Evans pitchers of this type are from a relatively small production, made c.1952 while he was still working as a "living craftsman" in Old Sturbridge Village, Massachusetts, before setting up shop in New Hope. 11in (28cm) high, **M**

The gentle curves and use of rosewood in this William Spratling coffee set give it an organic feel in keeping with Scandinavian Soft Modernism. Pot 6.75in (17cm) high, **M**

This brass and stainless steel coffee pot is one of the most iconic pieces Tommi Parzinger designed for American manufacturer Dorlyn. A matching milk jug and sugar pot were also available. 16.5in (42cm) high, **D**

The shape of this Paul Evans ashtray resembles a falling handkerchief – with riveted metal patchwork in copper, bronze, and pewter – a form that Paolo Venini and Fulvio Bianconi had great success within glass in the 1950s. 10in (25.5cm) wide, **F**

Poul Peterson

The decoration is confined to extremities. This is typical of Petersen's work.

The large flat area and matt-finish strongly echoes work produced at the Jensen studio during this period.

A Carl Paul Petersen silver tazza. c.1930. 10in (25.5cm) diam. **M**

The silverware made in Canada by Copenhagen-born Carl Poul Petersen (1895–1977) combines the elegant simplicity of Georg Jensen with elements of Art Nouveau. Petersen and his wife, who was the daughter of Jensen, moved to Montreal in 1929. After working for firms such as Henry Birks & Sons, he opened his own studio in 1944. Although his silverware was made using mechanical processes, it was usually hand-finished, often with *repoussé* decoration, giving it a luxurious, handmade feel. Today, Petersen's designs are housed in numerous museums around the world, including the Museum of Fine Arts, Montreal.

France, Germany, and Austria

The 1950s saw Parisian firm Christofle commissioning several pieces of avant-garde silver and electroplated tableware from Italian designers Lino Sabattini (b. 1925) and Gio Ponti (1891–1979). A Sabattini coffee pot has since proved to be one of his seminal works, now held in museum collections around the world. In Austria, designers such as Carl Auböck (1900–57) and Karl Dittert (b. 1915) designed simple, restrained forms for a range of companies including Amboss, Bruckmann & Söhne, and WMF. Germany's industry and industrial culture were slower to recover than those of other European countries, meaning there was less of a market for silverware. However, designers such as Carl Pott (1904–85) and Friedrich Becker (1922–97) produced many notable designs.

Cutlery designers in the mid-century broke away from traditional patterns and shapes: Carl Auböck created these minimalist knives and forks for Amboss in 1958. Knife 6.25in (16cm) long, **D** set of six

Lino Sabattini's "Bascule" silver coffeepot and milk jug from 1960 seem to have been influenced by Scandinavian designs. Teapot 4.75in (12cm) high, **I**

The fluid shape of this 1958 Bruckmann & Söhne coffee pot designed by Karl Dittert suggests the influence of Scandinavian silver, particularly the work of Johan Rohde for Georg Jensen. 10in (23.5cm) high, **H**

This 1960s candle sculpture by German company Nagel is made up of individual sections, which can be assembled into any combination. 4in (10cm) wide each, **D**

The brass form of this silver-plated brass "Cardinale" vase from 1957 is typical of the designs produced by Lino Sabattini for Christofle & Cie. 14.75in (37cm) high, **D**

Skyscrapers were a major source of design inspiration in the 1920s and 1930s, and the influence of that era can be seen in this silver-plated sculpture by Gio Ponti for Christofle & Cie. 13in (33cm) high, **M**

The steep angles of the spout and handle on this German silver coffee pot give the otherwise traditional shape a modern feel. Coffee pot 10in (27.5cm) high, 46oz (1.29 kg), **K**

Introduction: textiles

Left: Verner Panton's "Spectrum" designs for Mira-X inspired many other companies to produce wall hangings. The strong colours of this design from c.1975 were chosen to enhance Panton's furniture, creating a unified environment. 47.25in (120cm) wide, **K**

Right: Pierre Cardin believed in creating a homogeny between fashion and interior design. As a consequence he produced a range of textiles that echoed motifs used in his garments, such as the concentric circles of this Dekoplus fabric. 285in (724cm) long, 40in (101.5cm) wide, **D**

Reacting to drab Utility fashions, the textile designers of the mid-20th century created highly patterned and brightly coloured designs that soon gained them a reputation for individuality and invention. Today, the fabrics and rugs produced during this period are considered to be some of most innovative and memorable textiles of the 20th century.

Rather than traditional, realistic floral patterns, the textiles of the 1950s were more likely to depict seed heads, bark, twigs and leaves – a style that is exemplified by the work of Lucienne Day (1917–2010) for Heal & Son in London. The 1960s and 1970s saw the return of blossoms, which were depicted larger-than-life and in bright, block colours by designers such as Maija Isola (1927–2001) for Marimekko in Helsinki.

Other designers favoured geometric patterns over florals, or produced designs inspired by the scientific discoveries, popular culture, and art of the day. The work of artists such as Alexander Calder, Joan Miró, and Paul Klee was highly influential in the 1950s, with natural earth tones and primary colours being widely used. The 1960s saw designers turning to the Pop art of Andy Warhol and Op art of Bridget Riley for inspiration. So influential was modern art that many companies, including J. S. A. Busto Arsizio in Italy and Asher in the United Kingdom began commissioning textile designs by prominent artists such as Pablo Picasso.

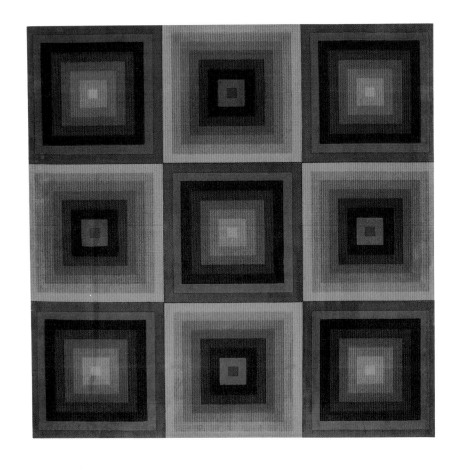

Leading furniture designers, including Arne Jacobsen (1902–71), Gio Ponti (1891–1979), Piero Fornasetti (1913–88), and Terence Conran (b. 1931), also began experimenting in textile design. One of the most prolific and successful was Verner Panton (1926–98), who created a range of fabrics and rugs for Swiss firm Mira-X in the 1960s and 1970s. Several of his designs were also produced as fabric wall hangings – a hugely popular idea that was taken up by many other companies, including Finlayson of Finland.

As well as the wall hanging, the mid-century brought another innovation to the world of textiles: the "area rug". More and more people, particularly in the United States, were living a transitory lifestyle, moving house frequently and leaving their fitted carpets behind. As a consequence, Raymond Loewy (1893–1986) created a series of five patterned rugs in collaboration with carpet manufacturer Edward Fields that were large enough to cover the floors of most living rooms. As the idea took off, other designers, such as Pierre Cardin (b. 1922), also created their own area rugs that were strongly influenced by the trends of the day.

Left: While many other 1950s designers were inspired by modern art, Piero Fornasetti, who designed these "Soli et Lune" curtains, took his inspiration from ancient artforms. 110in (282cm) long, **D**

Right: This English cloth is printed in typical 1950s colours. The stylization of the fruit brings to mind the work of Lucienne Day. 144in (366cm) long, 46in (117cm) wide, **B**

USA

A wide range of innovative textiles were designed in the USA during the 1950s and 1960s. These were produced both by small firms, mainly in and around Chicago, and by large furniture manufacturers such as Herman Miller and Knoll. Herman Miller fabrics of the 1950s are particularly notable due to the inspired appointment of Alexander Hayden Girard (1907–93) as director of the company's textile division. American fabric design in the 1960s was dominated by the bright, modern designs of Jack Lenor Larsen (b. 1927). Large area rugs became fashionable in the 1950s and many were made during the 1960s and 1970s.

Michael Graves believes that "there is an equity between the pragmatic function and the symbolic function". Dating from 1979, his abstract rug is on the cusp between Mid-Century Modern and Postmodernism. 86in (218.5cm) long, **K**

The warm colours and simple, graphic pattern of this fabric used to upholster this "Marshmallow" sofa are typical of Alexander Girard's textile designs. 51in (130cm) wide, **R**; **U** (sofa)

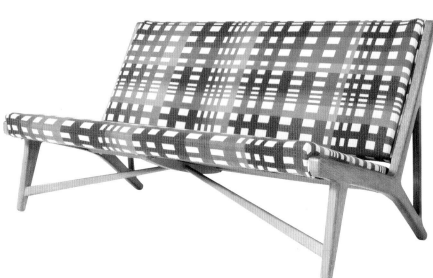

The Jack Lenor Larsen fabric used to upholster this Hans Wegner settee showcases the psychedelic colours of the 1960s. 58in (147.5cm) wide, **O**

This Edward Fields "Nutcracker Sweet" rug features a typically 1970s colour scheme. 100in (254cm) wide, **D**

The prototype tufting guns used by Edward Fields were not always reliable, but the resulting irregularities became one the company's signature traits. 80in (200cm) long, **J**

Circles and ellipses are extremely difficult to weave using traditional methods.

All Calder's tapestries are woven from native grasses dyed with vegetable colours.

This design, "Turquoise", is one of the most popular, as it strongly evokes Calder's famous mobiles.

An Alexander Calder "Turquoise" tapestry, 84.5in (215cm) long. U

In the early 1970s Alexander Calder (1898–1976), an artist best known for his mobiles, designed a range of limited-edition hammocks to benefit those affected by the devastating 1972 earthquake in Managua, Nicaragua. As well as having all the materials provided for them, the Nicaraguan weavers were also paid four times their normal wages for the work. Calder also designed 14 wall tapestries as part of the same charitable project. The tapestries, which were produced by artists in Guatemala, were limited to 100 examples of each design: "Floating Circles", "Turquoise", "Zebra", "Number Nine", "Sun", "Moon", "Star", "Circus", "Balloons", "Swirl", "Doll", "Pyramid", "Snake" and "Lombrizi".

Scandinavia

Refined fibres have often been in short supply in Scandinavia, leading to interior fabrics being regarded as the height of luxury and an art form in their own right. In the 1950s, many designers, including the influential Danish artist Lis Ahlmann (1894–1979), studied fine art before completing an apprenticeship in weaving and designing their own textiles. In Sweden, designers such as Elsa Gullberg (1886–1984) and Josef Frank (1885–1967) created many fabrics now considered design classics. The biggest Scandinavian success story belongs to the Finnish company Marimekko. Inspired by head designer Maija Isola (1927–2001), the company produced bright, larger-than-life patterns that epitomize the 1960s.

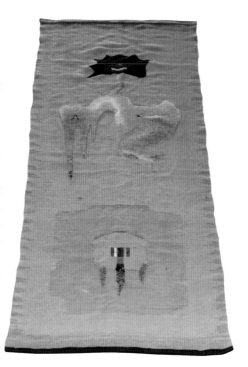

The pale ice colours used on this 1950s carpet are typical of mid-century Scandinavian designs in ceramic and glass. The red adds an unexpected accent. 122.5in (312.5cm) long, **M**

Highly stylized depictions of plant life are typical of 1950s patterns, as is the colour scheme of this Swedish fabric. 144in (366cm) long, **B**

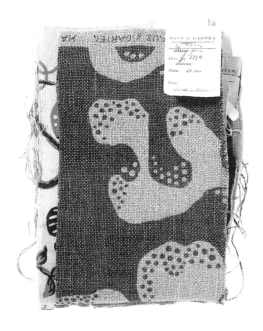

Josef Frank designed more than 125 fabric patterns, many of which are considered design classics. He was fascinated by exotic vegetation. Sample: **A**

This 1965 Verner Panton rug evokes the shapes produced by a Spirograph – a geometric drawing toy first popular in the mid-1960s. 88.5in (225cm) diam, **L**

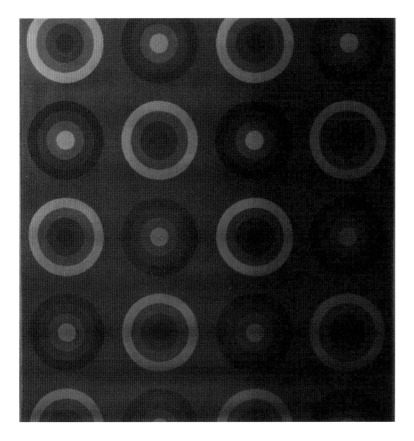

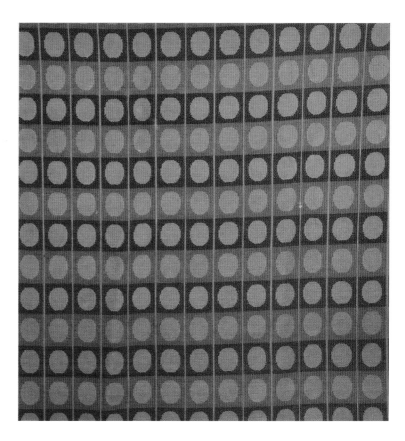

This Mira-X "Spectrum" area rug designed by Verner Panton around 1970 is clearly influenced by Op Art. 79.5in (202cm) wide, **J**

Although this Danish woven tapestry is made up of simple circles and lines, the pattern's optical effect adds dynamism. 108in (270cm) long, **G**

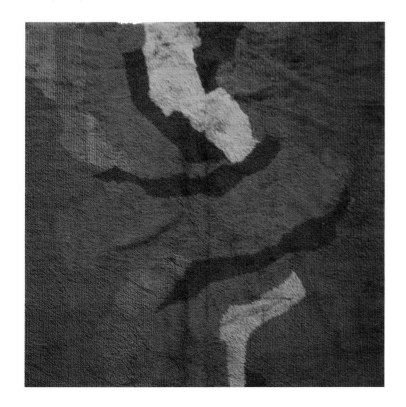

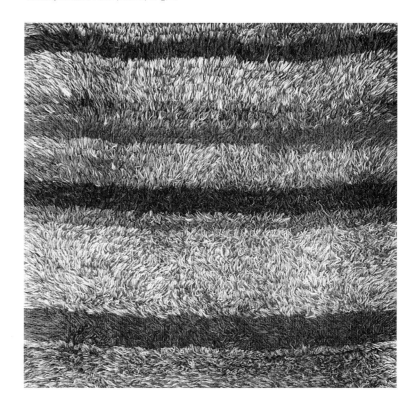

A "rya" is a Scandinavian wool rug with a long pile, traditionally used as a bed covering. Shag rugs and ryas, like this Danish example, were extremely fashionable in 1970s America. 137in (342.5cm) long, **D**

The mid-20th century saw a resurgence of the craft movement, which resulted in numerous hand-woven textile fabrics, including this Danish shag rug by Marianne Strengel. 90in (225cm) long, **H**

Britain

Under the directorship of Tom Worthington, the London-based furniture store Heal & Son was responsible for commissioning many of Britain's most memorable mid-century fabrics. Every year saw the introduction of around six new designs from Lucienne Day (see "A Closer Look"), as well as around 25 designs by a range of other talented designers. In the 1950s, the company's most high-profile designers included Michael O'Connell (1898–1976), Paule Vézelay (1892–1984), and Dorothy Carr, while the 1960s were dominated by Barbara Brown (b. 1939). Other notable British manufacturers of the period include David Whitehead and the Edinburgh Weavers, who produced designs created by artists such as the painters John Piper (1903–92) and Henry Moore (1898–1986).

In the 1950s, David Whitehead Fabrics established a reputation for contemporary design that was second only to that of Heal & Son. The company employed many leading artists and designers including Terence Conran, John Piper, and Henry Moore. Meter of fabric: **A**

The flat cartoon style of this yellow and brown fabric for Heal & Son, dating from 1964, is typical of the decade. 144in (366cm) long, **C**

Lucienne Day's designs became more architectural in the late 1950s and early 1960s. Strong patterns made up of plant silhouettes and columns of colour, such as "Larch" from 1961, are typical. 144in (366cm) long, **D**

The floral forms on this tapestry by Russian-born British architect and designer Serge Ivan Chermayeff have been simplified to the point of becoming geometric shapes. 76in (193cm) high, **L**

One of the most adventurous designers working for Heal & Son in the 1960s and 1970s, Barbara Brown inspired numerous later designers with her bold patterns. Meter of fabric: **A**

In the mid 1970s Heal & Son started to move from geometric patterns towards more floral designs, such as this "Poppies" fabric by Howard Carter. Other notable floral patterns by Mary Oliver and James Morgan were based on blown-up photographs. Meter of fabric: **A**

Lucienne Day

A panel of Heal & Son "Calyx" fabric, designed by Lucienne Day in 1951. 48.5in (123cm) wide. **H**

The "Calyx" print designed by Lucienne Day (1917–2010) is arguably the definitive fabric of the 1950s. Commissioned by Heal & Son, the fabric attracted significant attention after it was showcased at the 1951 Festival of Britain as part of two pavilions featuring Lucienne's textiles and her husband Robin's furniture. The highly stylized design was inspired by Scandinavian textiles and the work of painters such as Kandinsky and Klee. The spindly lines and curved shapes of "Calyx" perfectly complemented Robin's steel and plywood furniture. "Calyx" went on to win a multitude of international awards, including a gold medal at the 1951 Milan Triennale, and helped define a new look for post-war British textiles.

Other Europe

During the 1950s and 1960s, many European textile firms, notably including the Italian company J. S. A. Busto Arsizio, commissioned designs from high-profile artists. While many of these designs, including "I Cirri" by Gio Pomodoro (b. 1930), were abstract and painterly, Piero Fornasetti (1913–88) countered this trend by producing highly detailed figurative and architectural patterns. In the 1960s, Italy also saw the emergence of the fashion house founded by Emilio Pucci (1914–88), which produced a wide range of bold, diagonal patterns. The 1970s was a time of great creativity for German textile design, particularly from Stuttgarter Gardinenfabrik. The company's output was dominated by the designs of Antoinette de Boer (b. 1939), who also produced designs for her own company, De Boer Design, from 1973.

The colours of this Emilio Pucci scarf are more subtle than many of his designs, but the intricate pattern, composed on the diagonal, is typical of the "Prince of Prints". 50in (127cm) wide, **C**

Piero Fornasetti's designs are always highly detailed. The use of greys and blacks rather than bright colours sets his work apart from that of his contemporaries. 110in (279.5m) wide, **L**

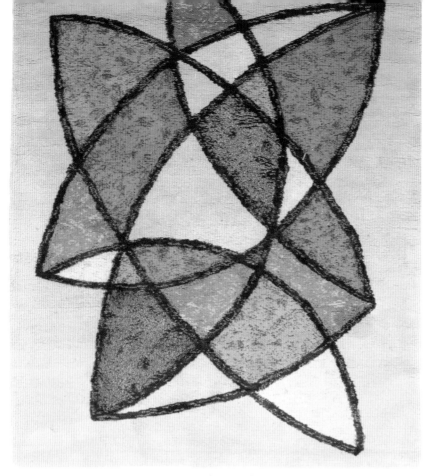

French designer Jacques Borker exhibited the first of the strongly coloured, geometric rugs he is now best known for in 1952. This example dates from c.1960. 81in (207cm) long, **D**

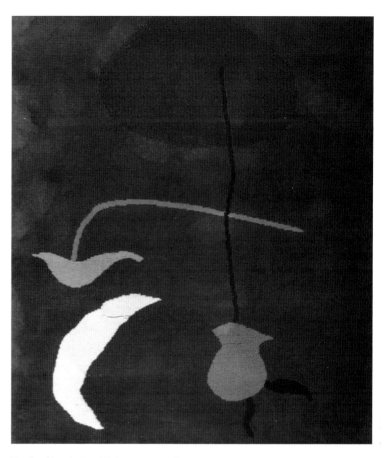

The Spanish artist Joan Miró was a major influence on many 1950s fabric designers. He also designed his own textiles, including this carpet, which strongly evokes his fine art work. 78in (198cm) long, **M**

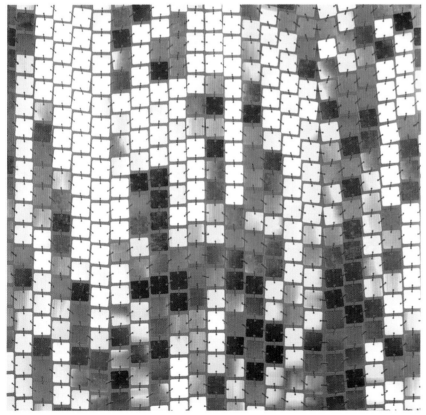

Designers in the 1960s and 1970s were strongly influenced by the idea of space travel and how people might live in the future. This early 1970s "Space-curtain" designed by Paco Rabanne is fabulously sci-fi. 78.74 in (200cm) long, 39in (99cm) wide, **F**

This carpet dating from around 1968 is typical of the work of Polish artist Zofia Butrymowicz. 81in (206cm) long, **H**

Designers

Alvar Aalto (1898–1976, Finland)

Aalto studied architecture at Helsinki University of Technology, setting up his own architecture practice in 1923. In 1935 he and his wife Aino founded a furniture manufacturing company, Artek. Aalto is best known for his bent plywood and laminated wood furniture, such as the cantilevered "No. 31" chair (1930–1).

Eero Aarnio (b. 1932, Finland)

A "Globe" chair, 1965

Aarnio graduated from the Institute of Industrial Arts in Helsinki in 1957 and established his own design office in 1962. His earliest designs featured natural materials and craft techniques, but in the 1960s he created space-age style fibreglass furniture, such as the "Ball" chair (1964–5).

Otl Aicher (1922–91, Germany)

Aicher established his own graphic design studio in 1948, having previously studied sculpture at the Munich Academy of Fine Arts. He was involved in the founding and development of the influential Ulm School of Design, which was open from 1953 until 1968. He worked with Dieter Rams at Braun in the 1950s, and is best known for his graphics for the 1972 Olympic Games in Munich.

A poster for the 1972 Munich Olympics

Tamara Aladin (b. 1932, Finland)

Aladin worked for Finnish glass manufacturer Riihimäen Lasi Oy from 1959 until 1976. Known for her undulating, mould-blown cased vases in bright colours, she was one of three female designers who `dominated the company's output during the 1960s.

A 1960s vase for Riihimaen Lasi Oy

Franco Albini *(1905–77. Italy)*

Albini studied architecture in Milan, graduating in 1929. He worked in the studio of Gio Ponti until 1930 when he established his own design and architectural practice. His designs, such as his suspension bookshelves of 1940, epitomize Italian Rationalism. He received Compasso d'Oro industrial design awards in 1955, 1958, and 1964.

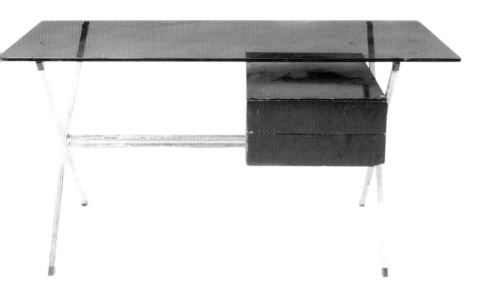

Jacob Bang *(1899–1965. Denmark)*

Having originally trained as an architect, Bang worked for Holmegaard glassworks from 1928 to 1941. He designed ceramics for Nymølle from 1936 onwards, and glassware for Kastrup from 1957 to 1965. Bang specialized in tableware, such as the "Primula" service (1930) for Holmegaard, and won several medals at world exhibitions, including at Barcelona in 1929.

Carl Auböck *(1900–57. Austria)*

After an apprenticeship in his father's metal workshop, Auböck studied at the Academy of Fine Arts in his native Vienna (1917–19), and at the Bauhaus in Weimar, Germany (1919–21). He took over the family business in 1925, making furniture and small household objects in brass, and went on to win four gold medals for his stylized metalware at the Milan Triennale in 1954.

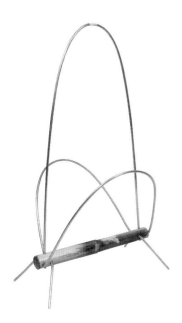

Michael Bang *(b. 1944. Denmark)*

The son of Jacob Bang, Michael Bang started designing glass for Holmegaard in 1968, having previously designed ceramics for Royal Copenhagen (1962–4), worked with Bjørn Wiinblad (1964–6), and designed glass for Ekenas Glasbruk (1966–8). His work for Holmegaard includes the opaque, brightly coloured "Palet" series (1970–5).

Ercol Barovier *(1889–1974, Italy)*

The Barovier family have made glass on the island of Murano since the 14th century. In 1919, Ercole Barovier founded his own workshop, Artisti Barovier (later Barovier e.C.) where he experimented with colours and techniques. He took over Fratelli Barovier, the family company, in 1936. From 1947 he worked with his son, Angelo, to create striped vessels known as *vetro a fili*.

Saul Bass *(1920–96, USA)*

Bass studied at the Art Students League of New York from 1936 to 1939, and worked for Warner Brothers until 1946. He set up his own office in Los Angeles in 1952, creating logos for companies such as United Airlines, and posters and title sequences for films such as *Vertigo* (1958).

Geoffrey Baxter *(1922–95, UK)*

Baxter joined Whitefriars Glass in 1954, straight after graduating from the Royal College of Art, London, where he was the first industrial designer to win a scholarship to the British School in Rome. Baxter is known for his Scandinavian-inspired, organically shaped vessels in modern colours. In 1967, he introduced his now iconic range of textured "bark" vases.

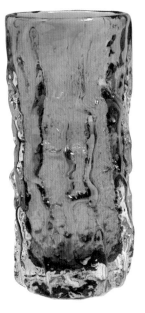

Herbert Bayer *(1900–85. Austria)*

Bayer studied mural painting at the Bauhaus school from 1921 to 1923, and started teaching there in 1925. From 1928, he led the Bauhaus workshop for printing and publicity and the advertising agency Dorland's Berlin studio. In 1938, he moved to the USA, where he worked as a design consultant for numerous companies.

Gerald Benney *(1930–2008. UK)*

Benney attended the Royal College of Art, London, in the early 1950s, and was Professor of Silversmithing there from 1974 to 1983. Known for his domestic silver with strong, simple lines and textured surfaces, he was appointed a Royal Designer for Industry in 1971. Benney received four Royal Warrants between 1974 and 1980.

Harry Bertoia *(1915–78. USA)*

Born in Italy, Bertoia emigrated to the United States in 1930. He studied at the Detroit School of Arts and the Cranbrook Academy of Art, Michigan in the late 1930s. He designed iconic furniture for Knoll, including the "Diamond Chair" (1952), still in production today.

Fulvio Bianconi *(1915–96. Italy)*

Raised in Venice, Bianconi worked at a Murano glass studio as a teenager, and went on to design perfume bottles in Milan. From 1948 to 1951 he designed figurines and vessels for Venini in Murano, including his famous "Fazzoletto" (handkerchief) vase.

Max Bill *(1908–94. Switzerland)*

Bill trained as a silversmith in Zurich in the mid 1920s before spending two years at the Bauhaus in Dessau. In the 1930s, he worked as a graphic designer, architect, and artist. He first produced industrial designs in 1944, and is known for pared-down products such as the "Ulmer Hocker" stool (1954). In the 1950s, he co-founded and taught at the Ulm School of Design.

Lubomir Blecha *(1933–2009. Czech Republic)*

A key figure in 20th-century Czech glass, Blecha came from a family of glassmakers, and trained at the College for Arts and Crafts in Prague before being accepted to study at the studio of Professor Josef Kaplického. He collaborated with several Czech glassworks, including Dobronín, Škrdlovice, and Novy Bor. In 1962 he moved to Slovakia, where he made organically shaped glass pieces.

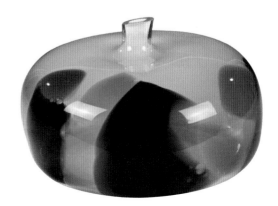

Cini Mariani Boeri *(b. 1924, Italy)*

Boeri studied architecture at the Polytechnic Institute of Milan, graduating in 1951. From 1952 to 1963, she worked in the design office of Marco Zanuso, and started designing furniture for Arflex in the mid-1960s. As well as furniture and showrooms for Knoll, Boeri has designed lighting for Artemide, Arteluce, Stinovo, and Venini.

Jiri Brabec *(1933–2005, Czech Republic)*

Brabec studied at the School of Applied Art at Turnov from 1948 to 1952, and the Academy of Applied Art in Prague from 1953 to 1959. He started designing press glass at the Rosice glassworks in 1965.

Osvaldo Borsani *(1911–85, Italy)*

After graduating from the Polytechnic Institute of Milan in 1937, Borsani worked for his father, an award-winning craftsman. In 1953 he and his brother founded a company, Tecno, manufacturing flexible, space-saving furniture of his own design. Suitable for post-war housing, products included the "D70" sofa, which turned into a bed (1954).

Otto Brauer *(Denmark)*

Brauer was appointed Master Glassblower at the Kastrup glassworks (later Kastrup-Holmegaard) in 1946. While working in this capacity he designed one of the company's most famous vessels, the "Gulvvase" (1962). The bottle-shaped vase was based on a 1958 design by Per Lütken.

Marcel Breuer *(1902–81, Hungary)*

Breuer briefly studied fine art in Vienna and worked in an architect's office before training in carpentry at the Bauhaus in Weimar (1920–23). He designed numerous private houses and interiors, as well as iconic pieces of furniture in tubular steel and bent plywood. In 1937 he moved to the USA to teach at Harvard's School of Design.

José Zanine Caldas *(1919–2011, Brazil)*

A self-taught artist, designer, and architect, Caldas set up a workshop in Rio at the age of 20, making scale models for architects including Oscar Niemeyer. In the 1940s, he created "Móveis Artísticos Z", a line of mass-produced plywood furniture. In the 1950s, he began making sculptural furniture, chiselled from logs.

Alexander Calder *(1898–1976, USA)*

After working as an engineer, Calder enrolled at the Art Students League of New York in 1923. In 1926 he moved to Paris, where he met avant-garde artists such as Joan Miró, before returning to the USA in 1933. He is known for his wire sculptures and kinetic artworks or "mobiles".

Anna Castelli Ferrieri *(1920–2006, Italy)*

From 1938 to 1943, Ferrieri studied architecture in Milan under Franco Albini. In 1943 she married Giulio Castelli, who founded the plastics manufacturing company Kartell in 1949. She began producing industrial designs (plastic homewares and furniture) in 1965, and was appointed design consultant for Kartell in 1966.

Livio *(1911–79, Italy)*
Pier Giacomo *(1913–68, Italy)*
and Achille Castiglioni *(1918–2002, Italy)*

The Castiglioni brothers graduated from the Polytechnic Institute of Milan in 1936, 1937, and 1944 respectively. Livio and Pier Giacomo set up a studio in 1938. Achille joined in 1944, while Livio left in 1952. As well as producing designs such as the "Arco" lamp (1962) and "Allunaggio" (moonlanding) seat (1966), they helped establish the Milan Triennale exhibitions and the ADI (*Associazione per il Disegno Industriale*).

Wendell Castle *(b. 1932, USA)*

Castle studied sculpture at the University of Kansas. In the 1960s, he experimented with fibreglass to produce sculptural furniture, such as the "Molar" chair (1969). In 1970, he started carving furniture from stack-laminated wood, turning to solid wood in 1976. In 1980, he founded the Wendell Castle Workshop to teach craftsmanship in wood.

John Clappison *(b. 1937, UK)*

Clappison was sponsored to attend the Royal College of Art in London by the founders of Hornsea Pottery. On graduating in 1958, he was made Chief Designer at the pottery. From 1972 to 1976, he designed glass for Ravenhead, before returning to Hornsea. In 1987, he became Chief Shape Designer at Royal Doulton.

Jean Cocteau *(1889–1963, France)*

Cocteau was a writer, designer, artist, and filmmaker. He met Pablo Picasso in 1915, and was strongly influenced by him. From 1957 to 1963, he created more than 300 ceramic objects at the workshops of artists Marie Madeline Jolly and Philippe Madeline in France.

Luigi Colani *(b. 1928, Germany)*

Colani studied fine art in Berlin in 1946 and aerodynamics in Paris from 1948. After working for aircraft manufacturer Douglas in California, he returned to Europe in 1954, where his clients included BMW and Rosenthal. He created playful but ergonomically sound furniture, such as the "*Körperform*" (body form) chair of 1973.

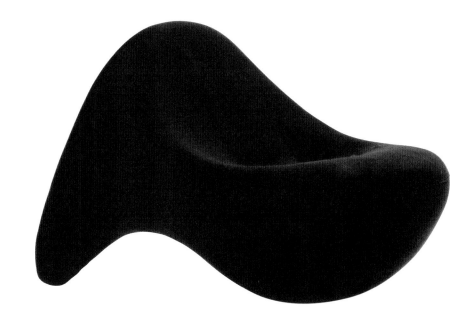

Joe Colombo *(1930–71, Italy)*

Colombo studied painting before training as an architect at the Polytechnic Institute of Milan until 1954, but he gave up art in favour of design around 1958. In 1959, he took over his father's electronics business, and began experimenting with new materials and techniques. He set up his own design office in Milan in 1962, producing classic designs such as the "Boby" trolley (1970).

Robin Day *(1915–2010, UK)*

Day graduated from the Royal College of Art, London, in 1938. In 1942, he married textile designer Lucienne Conradi, and they opened a design office in 1948. In 1949, he won MoMA's "International Competition for Low-Cost Furniture Design" with Clive Latimer. Day's "Polyprop" chair (1962–3) has sold more than 14 million units.

Terence Conran *(b. 1931, UK)*

Conran studied textile design at the Central School of Arts & Crafts, London, from 1949 to 1950. He set up his own furniture and textile design company in 1952 and co-founded the Conran Design Group (later Conran Associates) in 1956. In 1964, he opened the first Habitat store, selling well-designed products for modern homes.

Lucienne Day *(1917–2010, UK)*

Lucienne Conradi studied at the Croydon School of Art from 1934 to 1937 before attending the Royal College of Art, London. She married furniture designer Robin Day in 1942. Commissioned for the 1951 Festival of Britain, her extremely influential "Calyx" textile design was awarded a gold medal at the 1951 Milan Triennale. Day also won three Council of Industrial Design awards.

Stuart Devlin (b. 1931, UK)

Australian-born Devlin studied gold- and silversmithing at the Royal Melbourne Institute of Technology and at the Royal College of Art, London, in the late 1950s. In 1964, he designed Australia's first decimal coinage. He opened a workshop in London in 1965. In 1982, he was made Goldsmith to the Queen, and from 1996 to 1997 he was Prime Warden of the Goldsmiths' Company.

Nanna Ditzel (1923–2005, Denmark)

Nanna Hauberg studied furniture design at the School of Arts and Crafts in Copenhagen, where she met her husband, Jørgen Ditzel, with whom she collaborated until his death in 1961. She initially focused on design for small spaces and furniture, but also designed jewellery for Georg Jensen in the 1950s. Ditzel went on to also design metalware, tableware, and textiles.

Carlo di Carli (1910–71, Italy)

An architect and designer, di Carli worked with Gio Ponti in the 1940s and 1950s. In 1957, he founded the review *Il Mobile Italiano*, with the aim of documenting the work of Italy's furniture designers and makers. He also worked with design students in Milan and Turin.

Charles (1908–78, USA)
and Ray Eames (1912–88, USA)

Charles Eames trained as an architect, opening an office in 1930. In 1939, he joined the faculty of the Cranbrook Academy of Art, where he met Ray Kaiser, a student of weaving. The couple moved to California, and began working on innovative moulded plywood products. Herman Miller started producing their designs in 1949.

Tom Eckersley *(1914–97, UK)*

On leaving Salford School of Art in 1934, Eckersley set up an office in London with Eric Lombers. They designed graphics for clients including London Transport, the General Post Office, and the BBC. During World War II, Eckersley designed public information posters, for which he was awarded an OBE in 1949.

Leslie Elsden *(UK)*

Elsden joined Poole Pottery in the early 1950s. Elsden experimented with and perfected the technique of spray glazing vases, becoming head of the spraying shop. He is best known for creating the "Aegean" range, introduced in 1970. It utilizes spray-on glazes in a wide range of techniques and patterns, from abstract to more figural.

Egon Eiermann *(1904–70, Germany)*

Trained at the Technical University of Berlin (1923–7), Eiermann was a key figure in post-war German architecture, famous for the Kaiser Wilhelm Memorial Church (1959–63) in Berlin, as well as an influential furniture designer. He was a founding member of the German Design Council (*Rat für Formgebung*) in 1951, and his woven rattan armchair (1949) was featured in the German pavilion he designed with Sepp Ruff for Expo 58.

Wharton Esherick *(1887–1970, USA)*

After studying fine art in his native Philadelphia until 1909, Esherick worked as an illustrator and painter. He began working with wood in 1919, making woodcuts and small sculptures. In the 1920s, he started to apply the principles of sculpture to furniture, and took on Rudolph Steiner's "organic functionalist" design ideas. By the late 1930s, he had developed his own distinctive organic style.

Paul Evans *(1931–87, USA)*

Evans studied at the Philadelphia Textile Institute, the Rochester Institute of Technology, the School for American Craftsmen, and the Cranbrook Academy of Art. He began making sculptural metal furniture in the 1950s. From 1964 he designed for Directional Furniture, combining handcraft and technology in furniture lines such as the "Argente" and "Cityscape" series.

Marcello Fantoni *(1915–2011, Italy)*

From 1927 to 1934, Fantoni studied at the Institute of Art at Porta Romana, Florence. He established his own ceramic studio in 1936. His ceramics, which were distributed in the US by Raymor, embraced modern art and his Italian heritage. In 1970 Fantoni founded the International School of Ceramic Arts in Florence.

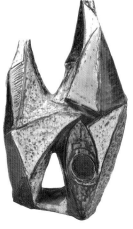

Piero Fornasetti *(1913–88, Italy)*

Fornasetti studied at Milan's Brera Academy of Fine Art from 1930 to 1932. In the 1930s he designed glass for Venini, and posters and covers for *Domus* and *Graphus* magazines. In 1940, he started working with Gio Ponti, collaborating on interiors and furniture decorated with his signature surreal, neo-Classical motifs.

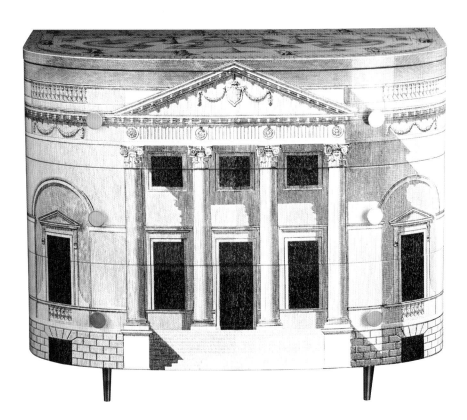

Kaj Franck (1911–89, Finland)

A pair of Arabia salt and pepper shakers

Franck studied furniture design at the University of Art and Design, Helsinki. He graduated in 1932, and started designing textiles at the Hyvinkää United Wool Factory in 1938. In 1945, he began working for ceramics company Arabia, becoming art director in 1950. His glass designs were produced by Iittala and Nuutajärvi-Notsjö.

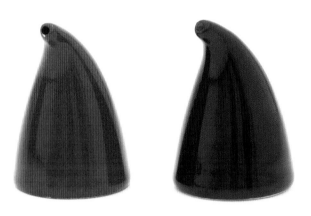

Abram Games (1914–96, UK)

A Festival of Britain car badge, 1951

After abandoning the commercial art course at St Martin's School of Art, London, Games worked in a graphic studio, setting up on his own in 1935. During World War II, he was the War Office's official poster artist, and later worked for London Transport and the Post Office. He is best known for his emblem for the 1951 Festival of Britain.

Guido Gambone (1909–69, Italy)

A decorated charger

Gambone worked as apprentice and then painter at Avallone ceramics in Vietri on the Amalfi Coast, before moving to MACS (*Manifattura Artistica Ceramica Salernitana*), and ICS (*Industria Ceramica Salernitana*). He became artistic director of ICS in 1935. After World War II, he co-founded a ceramics factory, Faenzarella. In 1950 he moved to Florence and founded Tirrena.

Peter Ghyczy (b. 1940, Hungary/Germany)

"Garden Egg Chair"

Born in Budapest, Ghyczy studied architecture at the Technical University of Aachen, Germany. In the late 1960s, he began working at Elastogran, where he designed many products in polyurethane, including the "Garden Egg Chair" (1967–8). He founded Ghyczy & Co. Design in Viersen, Germany, in 1972, and moved the office to the Netherlands in 1974.

Alexander Hayden Girard *(1907–93, USA)*

Raised in Italy, Girard studied architecture in Rome and London before moving to New York in 1932. He ran his own design studio in Detroit from the mid 1930s, and moved to Santa Fe in the early 1950s. Known for his colourful, exuberant home furnishings, he was appointed director of Herman Miller's textile division in 1952.

David Hammond *(b. 1931, UK)*

Hammond was apprenticed to Thomas Pitchford, one of the chief designers at Webb Crystal in Stourbridge, England. After joining the company in 1947, he worked in a variety of traditional and modern styles, and often combined different techniques, such as intaglio with engraving. In the early 1960s, he designed the "Flair" range with Stanley Eveson, which often featured controlled bubbles in the base of the vessels.

Greta Magnusson Grossman

(1906–99, Sweden)

Grossman completed a woodworking apprenticeship in the late 1920s before attending Stockholm's School of Art and Design. She co-founded a store/workshop in Stockholm in 1933, and moved to Los Angeles in 1940. She designed pioneering lamps for Barker Brothers in the late 1940s, and went on to design sophisticated furniture for numerous companies, including Glenn of California.

Václav Hanus *(1924–2009, Czech Republic)*

After first studying jewellery making, Hanus attended the Academy of Applied Art in Prague from 1945 to 1949. He designed cut and pressed glass for the Inwald glassworks from 1955 to 1956, the Rudolfova glassworks from 1957 to 1960, and joined the Jablonec glassworks in 1960.

Jiri Harcuba *(b. 1928, Czech Republic)*

Harcuba learned engraving at the Harrachov glassworks in the early 1940s. He trained at the Specialized School of Glassmaking in Nový Bor from 1945 to 1948, and then at the Academy of Applied Arts in Prague, where he went on to teach from 1961 to 1971. He is known for his portraiture in engraved glass.

Michael Harris *(1933–94, UK)*

Harris studied glass design at the Royal College of Art, London, from 1956 to 1960, and became a tutor of Industrial Glass there in 1963. He left the RCA in 1968 to set up Mdina Glass on Malta. He went on to found Isle of Wight Studio Glass in 1973. Harris is known for his Mediterranean-inspired colours.

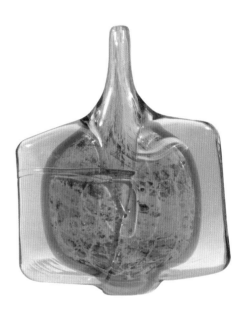

Alexander Hardie Williamson

(1907–94, UK)

Hardie Williamson studied lithography and commercial design at Harrogate School of Arts and Crafts, and textiles at the Royal College of Art, London, graduating in 1932. He taught at the Royal College from 1933 to 1955. In 1944 he joined United Glass, and produced more than 1700 designs for its subsidiaries Sherdley and Ravenhead.

Poul Henningsen *(1894–1967, Denmark)*

Henningsen studied architecture in Copenhagen from 1911 to 1917. After working as a journalist for eight years, he started designing lighting for Louis Poulsen in 1924. The first lamp from his celebrated "PH" series was shown at the landmark Paris exhibition of decorative arts in 1925. He produced more than 100 designs for lamps, while also continuing his career in journalism.

Frédéric Henri Kay Henrion

(1914–90, Germany)

Born in Nuremberg, Henrion studied graphic design in Paris in the 1930s before moving to the UK in 1936, where he designed wartime posters utilizing Dada-style photo-montage for the Ministry of Information. He worked on the 1951 Festival of Britain and went on to specialize in corporate identity design for clients such as KLM.

Erik Höglund *(1932–2001, Sweden)*

Höglund studied at Stockholm's University College of Art, Craft and Design from 1948 to 1953, and at various institutions around Europe and the USA. From 1953 to 1973, he designed highly influential pieces for the Boda glassworks, Sweden. In the late 1970s and 1980s, he collaborated with various other glassworks, notably Studioglas Strömbergshyttan.

Pavel Hlava *(1924–2003, Czech Republic)*

Between 1939 and 1948, Hlava studied at the Železný Brod glass school and the Academy of Applied Art, Prague. Known for his highly experimental pieces, from 1948 to 1959 he worked with the Czech Centre of Design in the Glass and Ceramic Industry, and at the Institute of Interior and Fashion Design, Prague, from 1959 to 1985.

Josef Hospodka *(1923–89, Czech Republic)*

Hospodka studied at the Graphic Art School, Prague, from 1938 to 1940, and then at the city's School of Industrial Art from 1940 to 1944. From 1945 to 1951 he ran the cutting department at the glass school at Novy Bor. In 1958 he became the head designer at Borské Sklo glassworks. He is best known for his free-blown designs.

Maija Isola (1927–2001, Finland)

Isola studied painting at Helsinki's University of Art and Design from 1946 to 1949. On graduating, she became the principle designer for textile firm Printex, and in 1951, she began designing for Printex's sister company, Marimekko. She is best known for her bold geometric patterns, such as the huge, bright poppies of "Unikko" (1964).

Arata Isozaki (b. 1931, Japan)

Isozaki studied at the University of Tokyo under Brutalist architect Kenzo Tange, with whom he continued to work into the 1970s. He established his own office in 1963 and took part in many notable architectural projects. Isozaki's product designs combine Eastern and Western influences, namely Japanese art, Postmodernism, and popular culture.

Arne Jacobsen (1902–1971, Denmark)

After training as a mason, Jacobsen studied at the Royal Danish Academy of Fine Arts in Copenhagen, graduating in 1927. He is best known for his sculptural chair designs, which include the "Series 7" (1955) and the "Swan" and "Egg" chairs (both 1957–8). He designed lighting for Louis Poulsen, metalware for Stelton and Michelsen, and worked on architectural projects.

Pierre Jeanneret (1896–1967, Switzerland)

Jeanneret trained as an architect in Geneva. In 1922 he joined the office of his cousin, Le Corbusier, in Paris and co-designed an influential range of furniture with him and Charlottle Perriand, including the "B306" *chaise-longue* (1928). He also designed furniture independently and worked on prefabricated housing with Jean Prouvé.

Robert Jefferson (b. 1929, UK)

Jefferson, formerly a ceramics lecturer at Stoke-on-Trent College of Art, joined Poole Pottery as a designer in 1958. In 1961 he and Guy Sydenham re-launched the Poole Studio, with Jefferson decorating many of the pieces. He was also responsible for the "Delphis" range (1963).

Vladimir Jelinek *(b. 1934, Czech Republic)*

From 1949 to 1958, Jelinek studied at the glass school at Kamenicky Senov and then at Prague's Academy of Applied Art. He designed for the Karolinka glassworks from 1961 to 1964 and the Institute of Interior and Fashion Design from 1964 to 1977 and from 1981 to 1998. Jelinek also produced glass in association with Skrdlovice, Novy Bor, and Moser.

Finn Juhl *(1912–89, Denmark)*

Juhl studied architecture at the Royal Danish Academy of Fine Art in Copenhagen, graduating in 1934. In the following decade he designed furniture with Niels Vodder, before opening his own office in 1945. He designed sculptural, beautifully crafted furniture, including the "Chieftain" chair (1949), and helped popularize the use of teak in Danish design.

A "Model 57" sofa, 1957

Georges Jouve *(1910–64, France)*

Jouve studied sculpture, painting, and art history in Paris. After graduating in 1930, he worked as a set designer. During World War II, he escaped from a prisoner-of-war camp and hid in Dieulefit, a potters' village in the south of France, where he learned the local craft. In 1945, he opened a ceramics studio in Paris. In the late 1950s, he abandoned ceramics and turned to sculpture.

A ceramic vase with applied plaque

Rudolf Jurnikl *(1928–2010, Czech Republic)*

Jurnikl studied at the glass school at Kamenicky Senov from 1945 to 1948, and at the Academy of Applied Art, Prague, from 1948 to 1953. He worked at the Rudolfova glassworks from 1960, where he largely produced pressed glass designs.

A Rudolfova glassworks vase, 1963

Vladimir Kagan (b. 1927. Germany)

A glass-topped occasional table

Born in Germany, Kagan moved to the United States with his family in 1938. He studied architecture at Columbia University and learned cabinet-making in his father's workshop. He opened a shop in New York in 1949, and his clients ranged from Marilyn Monroe to General Motors. His designs are sculptural, curvaceous, and organic.

Miloslav Klinger (1922–99. Czech Republic)

A Zelezny Brod Alexandrite glass vase, 1964

Having trained in lampworking techniques, Klinger studied at the Zelezny Brod glass school from 1938 to 1941 and the Academy of Applied Art in Prague from 1942 to 1948. From 1948 to 1982, he was the head designer at the Zelezny Brod glassworks, where he designed free-formed figurines and sculptural glass.

Poul Kjærholm (1929–80. Denmark)

A pair of "PK22" lounge chairs

Having trained as a carpenter, Kjærholm studied furniture design and cabinet-making at the School of Arts and Crafts, Copenhagen. His elegant furniture, such as the "PK22" chair (1955), was designed to be mass-produced, and was mainly manufactured by E. Kold Christensen and later by Fritz Hansen. He taught at the Royal Danish Academy of Fine Art, Copenhagen, for more than 20 years.

Florence Knoll (b. 1917. USA)

A Knoll table desk, 1961

Florence Schust studied architecture at the Cranbrook Academy of Art, Michigan, and at the Architectural Association in London. She joined Hans Knoll's furniture company in 1943, becoming his wife and business partner in 1946, when they formed Knoll Associates. She pioneered the distinctive Modern Knoll look and the company's innovative approach to space planning.

Mogens Koch (1898–1993. Denmark)

Koch trained as an architect at the Royal Danish Academy of Fine Arts, graduating in 1925. He worked as an assistant to Carl Petersen and Kaare Klint, who influenced his work. Koch's designs – subtly updated variations of tried and tested forms – were manufactured by Interna, Rudolf Rasmussen, and Danish CWS, among others.

Henning Koppel (1918–81. Denmark)

Koppel studied drawing and sculpture in Copenhagen from 1935 to 1937, and spent 1938 studying in Paris. He began designing gold and silver jewellery in the 1940s, and went on to work with Georg Jensen from 1946 until his death, producing sculptural silver vessels as well as jewellery. Koppel also designed glassware, ceramics, clocks, lighting, and postage stamps.

Yrjö Kukkapuro (b. 1933. Finland)

Kukkapuro studied at the Institute of Industrial Arts, Helsinki, graduating in 1958. In 1959 he established his own studio and began designing functionalist furniture, inspired by the work of Ilmari Tapiovaara. His designs were manufactured by Haimi until 1980, and then by Avarte. In 1974, the *New York Times* named his "Karusseli" chair (1965) the most comfortable chair in the world.

Nils Landberg *(1907–91, Sweden)*

Landberg studied at the School of Applied Arts in Gothenburg from 1923 to 1925, then at the Orrefors engraving school. He began designing for Orrefors in 1935, initially creating engraved glassware. In the 1950s, he experimented with stretched and abstract forms in clean or delicately tinted glass. His "Tulpanglas" (1957) won a gold medal at the Milan Triennale.

Jack Lenor Larsen *(b. 1927, USA)*

Larsen studied architecture and furniture design in Seattle and Los Angeles, graduating in 1950, and completed a master's degree in fine art at Cranbrook Academy of Art. He established a weaving studio in Seattle in 1949, and his own workshop in New York in 1951. He is known for designing innovative machine-woven textiles that look as if they were made by hand.

Le Corbusier *(1887–1965, Switzerland)*

Charles-Édouard Jeanneret, who adopted the pseudonym Le Corbusier around 1920, built his first house in his native Switzerland aged 18. He set up an architectural partnership with his cousin, Pierre Jeanneret, in Paris in 1922. The functional tubular steel furniture he began designing in collaboration with Jeanneret and Charlotte Perriand in 1927 epitomizes the International Style.

Stanislav Libenský *(1921–2002, Czech Republic)*

Libenský studied at the glass school in Nový Bor, at Železný Brod, and at the Prague Academy of Arts, Architecture and Design, graduating in 1944. In 1953 he became director of the Železný Brod glass school, where he met Jaroslava Brychtová. The couple, who married in 1963, are known for their optical glass sculptures.

Roy Lichtenstein *(1923–97, USA)*

Lichtenstein studied and later taught art at Ohio State University. He started teaching at Rutgers University, New Jersey, where he was influenced by Allan Kaprow, in 1960. In 1961 he created his first Pop art paintings using cartoon and commercial printing imagery. As well as paintings, he made metal and plastic sculptures.

Stig Lindberg *(1916–82, Sweden)*

Lindberg studied in Jönköping and Stockholm, and briefly in Paris. He started working at Gustavsberg ceramics in 1937, becoming artistic director in 1949. In the 1940s and 1950s, he also designed glassware for Maleras and Holmegaard, and textiles for Nordiska. He left Gustavsbersg in 1957 to take up a teaching post, but returned to work at the company from 1971 to 1980.

Otto Lindig *(1895–1966, Germany)*

Lindig studied sculpture at the College of Fine Arts in Weimar, graduating in 1918. In 1919, he enrolled at the newly established Bauhaus, Weimar, where he studied ceramics. Going on to run the school's ceramic workshop, he strongly influenced Bauhaus ceramics, combining handcraft with mass-production techniques.

An earthenware vase

Vicke Lindstrand *(1904–83, Sweden)*

Lindstrand studied graphic design at the Swedish Arts and Crafts Association School in Gothenburg. He designed glass for Orrefors from 1928 to 1941 while also producing designs for the Karlskrona porcelain factory and ceramics manufacturer Upsala-Ekeby, where he took on the role of art director in 1943. As well as running his own studio, he was also design director at Kosta Boda from 1950.

A Kosta glass vase, c.1952

Raymond Loewy *(1893–1986, France)*

After studying engineering in France, Loewy moved to the USA in 1919. He worked as a fashion illustrator before setting up his own industrial design office in New York in 1929 and the influential Raymond Loewy Associates in 1944. He is known for designing streamlined vehicles and the packaging of Lucky Strikes (1942), and for redesigning Air Force One for John F. Kennedy.

A Rosenthal "Birdcage" coffee pot and sugar bowl

Ingeborg Lundin *(1921–92, Sweden)*

Lundin joined Orrefors in 1947, becoming the company's first female designer. During the 1950s she designed her "Äpplet" art object, which has been described as the "world's best known pieces of 1950s glass". She is remembered for her engraved glass, made using the "Arial" technique previously developed at Orrefors.

Per Lütken *(1916–98, Denmark)*

Lütken trained as a painter at the School of Arts and Crafts in Copenhagen. He worked for Holmegaard from 1942 to 1998, during which time he created a wide range of designs, from one-off sculptural glass to mass-produced domestic tableware. He also designed most of Holmegaard's promotional material.

A "Carnaby" vase for Holmegaard, c.1960

Vico Magistretti *(1920–2006, Italy)*

Magistretti studied architecture in Lausanne and Milan, and designed his first pieces of Modernist-style furniture in 1946. His "Caremate" (1959) chair, a modern take on the traditional rush-seated chair, was mass-produced by Cassina from 1962. In the 1960s, he began working with plastic, creating designs such as the "Stadio" table (1965).

A set of "Caremate" chairs, 1959

Angelo Mangiarotti *(b. 1921, Italy)*

Mangiarotti studied at Milan's Polytechnic Institute. After graduating in 1948, he worked and taught in the USA, returning to Italy in 1955. He worked as a design consultant with Bruno Morassutti until 1960, when he started working as an independent architect and designer for manufacturers including Knoll and Zanotta.

A "P106-section" table clock, 1956

Gerhard Marcks *(1861–1981, Germany)*

A self-taught sculptor, Marcks was made artistic director of the Bauhaus's ceramic workshop in 1920. He left in 1924 to run the sculpture workshop at a college in Halle, but was forced out by the Nazi regime in 1933. The highly rational designs he produced during the 1920s and 1930s were suited to mass production. Following World War II, he taught sculpture in Hamburg before moving to Cologne in 1950, where he continued his work as an artist.

Enzo Mari *(b. 1932, Italy)*

Mari studied classics and literature at the Brera Acadamy of Fine Art in Milan, graduating in 1956. In 1957, he began working with plastic products manufacturer Danese. A thoughtful and influential design theorist, he went on to design experimental products and furniture for companies such as Zanotta, Driade, and Castelli.

Bruno Mathsson *(1907–88, Sweden)*

After an apprenticeship in the family cabinet-making business, Mathsson started experimenting with and designing innovative bentwood furniture in the early 1930s. His later collaboration with the mathematician Piet Hein resulted in products such as the "Superellipse" table (1964), manufactured by Fritz Hansen.

Dino Martens *(1894–1970, Italy)*

Martens studied painting at the Academy of Fine Art in Venice, and worked as a painter for several Muranese glassworks during the 1920s and 1930s. In 1939 he became artistic director of Aureliano Toso, where he developed his influential "Oriente" and "Zanfrico" ranges, and held the position until 1965.

Adolf Matura *(1921–79, Czech Republic)*

Between 1938 and 1947, Matura studied at the Železný Brod glass school, the School of Decorative Arts in Prague, and the Prague Academy of Applied Art. Known for his glass tableware, he worked with the Centre for the Glass and Ceramics Industry and designed pieces for the Institute of Interior and Fashion Design in Prague.

Paul McCobb *(1917–69, USA)*

McCobb had no formal training when he set up his own design company in 1945. He worked in furniture retail and display before launching the "Planner Group" line of simple, moderately priced, modular furnishings in 1950. It stayed in production until 1964. Between 1950 and 1955, he was awarded MoMA's Good Design Award five times.

A "Planner Group" chest of drawers, 1950s

Ludwig Mies Van der Rohe

(1886–1969, Germany)

A former apprentice of architect Peter Behrens, Mies set up an office in Berlin in 1912. In 1927, he designed his first tubular metal chair, the "MR10", with Lilly Reich. He was director of the Bauhaus from 1930 to 1933. After moving to the USA in 1937, he focused on architecture.

"Brno" armchair, 1930

David Mellor *(1930–2009, UK)*

A craftsman and a design entrepreneur, Mellor trained as a silversmith at Sheffield College of Art and the Royal College of Art, London, graduating in 1954. He is known for designing and manufacturing stainless steel and silver flatware, such as "Embassy" (1963), designed for British embassies, and the "Thrift" range (1965), which was used in a wide variety of public institutions.

A set of cutlery from the "Pride" range, 1953

Børge Mogensen *(1914–72, Denmark)*

From 1936 to 1941, Mogensen studied at the School of Arts and Crafts in Copenhagen and with Kaare Klint at the Royal Danish Academy of Fine Arts. He set up his own studio in 1950 and designed for companies including Søborg Møbelfabrik. He is known for re-interpreting traditional shapes, such as his "Spanish" chair (1959).

A 2431 armchair, 1972

Carlo Mollino *(1905–73. Italy)*

An "Elbow" chair with ottoman. 1959

The son of an architect and engineer, Mollino studied engineering and art history before gradating from Turin's School of Architecture in 1931. Inspired by Surrealism and Futurism, his furniture is typically biomorphic in shape and often designed for specific sites. Mollino's distinctive and exuberant style became known as "Turinese Baroque".

Olivier Mourgue *(b. 1939. France)*

A "Djinn" chair. 1965

From 1954 to 1961, Mourgue studied interior and furniture design in Paris, Sweden, and Finland. After working for French manufacturer Airborne International, where he designed the sculptural "Djinn" seating range (1965), Mourgue established his own studio in 1966, designing furniture as well as interiors and living environments.

Serge Mouille *(1922–88. France)*

A "Tripod" lamp. c1954

Mouille trained as a silversmith at the School of Applied Arts in Paris, graduating in 1941. The prototype three-armed standard lamp he designed in 1953 for Jacques Adnet was the first of many elegant lamps with adjustable metal shades he produced until 1962. Mouille thought of his handmade lamps as art, like his work as a silversmith.

George Nakashima *(1905–90. USA)*

An early 1960s dining chair

Nakashima studied architecture in Seattle and at M.I.T. After graduating in 1930, he worked in India and Japan for architect Antonin Raymond. While interned in a US camp from 1942 to 1943, he learned traditional Japanese carpentry. In 1946, he set up a "craft furniture" studio in New Hope, Pennsylvania. He also designed for Knoll.

George Nelson (1907–86, USA)

A "Bubble" lamp, 1947

Nelson studied architecture and art at Yale until 1931, before attending the American Academy in Rome. From 1935, he wrote for *Architectural Form* and *Pencil Points*, introducing European Modernism to the USA. He was director of design at Herman Miller from 1946 to 1972, working with Charles Eames and Isamo Naguch.

Isamu Noguchi (1904–88, USA)

Born in Los Angeles, Noguchi spent part of his childhood in Japan. After quitting medical school, he studied sculpture in New York in the early 1920s. From 1927 to 1929 he was an assistant to Constantin Brancusi in Paris. On returning to the USA in 1932, Noguchi focused on sculpture, but also designed glassware for Steuben, furniture for Herman Miller and Knoll, and paper lamps.

Gunnar Nylund (1904–89, Sweden)

A Rörstrand porcelain bowl

Nylund studied architecture before joining Bing & Grøndahl in Copenhagen in 1926. In 1929 he established Saxbo with Nathalie Krebs. He left in 1930 to work for Rörstrand until 1958, where he designed the subtly glazed pottery for which he is known. In the 1960s he designed ceramics for Nymølle and glass for Strömbergshyttan.

Gunnel Nyman (1909–48, Finland)

A Nuutajärvi Notsjo "Helmihuulu" (string of pearls) vase, late 1940s

Nyman trained at the Central School of Art and Design, Helsinki. She designed furniture, textiles, wallpaper, ceramics, and silver, but is best known as Finland's leading glass designer. In her short career, she freelanced for Riihimäki (1932–47), Karhula (1935–7), and Iittala (1946–7), producing extremely succesful designs.

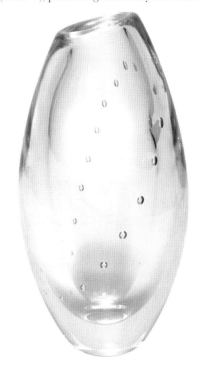

Sven Palmqvist *(1906–84. Sweden)*

After five years as a glass- and mould-maker at Hjertsö glassworks, Palmqvist joined the Orrefors engraving school in 1927. He worked for Orrefors as an assistant from 1928, and as a designer from 1936. Palmqvist invented the "Ravenna" and "Kraka" techniques there in the 1940s, and perfected centrifuge casting in 1954.

Tommi Parzinger *(1903–81. Germany/USA)*

After studying at the Munich School of Arts and Crafts, Parzinger moved to New York in 1935. He designed ceramics, glass, and furniture for Rena Rosenthal, and furniture for Charak of Boston from 1938. In 1939 he opened his first showroom, Parzinger Inc. (later Parzinger Originals). His furniture was often covered in lacquer, leather, or wood veneer, and featured metal details.

Verner Panton *(1926–98. Denmark)*

Panton graduated from Royal Danish Academy of Fine Arts, Copenhagen, in 1951. From 1950 to 1952 he worked for Arne Jacobsen, and established his own design studio in 1955. As well as furniture, he designed seating, lighting, textiles, carpets, and exhibition installations, all of which were innovative, bold, and playful.

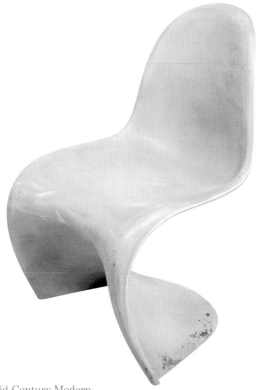

Pierre Paulin *(1927–2009. France)*

Paulin studied stone-carving and clay modelling in Paris. He started designing furniture for Thonet in 1954, and Artifort from 1958. In the mid 1960s, he started his own design office in Paris, where he designed sculptural foam-upholstered furniture such as his "Ribbon" chair (1965) and "Tongue" chair (1967).

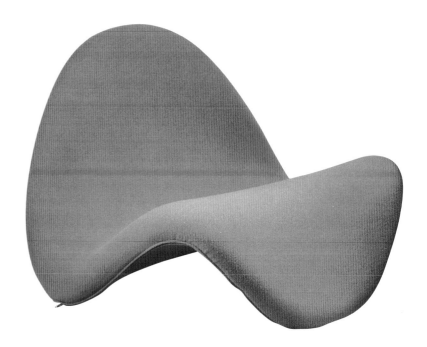

František Pecený (1920–77, Czech Republic)

A Sklo Union pressed glass vase, 1961

Pecený studied at the glass school at Železný Brod from 1936 to 1939 and at the School of Industrial Art from 1939 to 1943. He designed ceramics for Amphora from 1945 to 1946 and pressed glass for Hermanova glassworks from 1947 to 1977.

Charlotte Perriand (1903–99, France)

Perriand studied at the School of the Central Union of Decorative Arts in Paris from 1920 to 1925. From 1927 to 1937, she worked with Le Corbusier and Pierre Jeanneret, producing revolutionary tubular steel furniture in the Modern style. In 1940, she set up an architectural office with Jeanneret, Jean Prouvé, and Georges Blanchon.

Gaetano Pesce (b. 1939, Italy)

An "Up" sofa 1969

Pesce studied architecture and industrial design in Venice, graduating in 1965. He went on to produce highly innovative furniture and interior designs for companies such as the "Up" series (1969) of chairs for C&B Italia (known as B&B Italia since 1974), Cassina, and Venini. Pesce is known for his exploration of new materials and production techniques, and his sense of humour.

Pablo Picasso *(1881–1973, Spain)*

Picasso rejected formal education and moved to Paris in 1900. By 1905 he had become a favourite of art collector and poet, Gertrude Stein, and in 1907 he joined Daniel-Henry Kahnweiler's art gallery. Picasso is best known for pioneering the Cubist movement with George Braque. He also contributed towards significant developments in sculpture, print-making, and ceramics.

John Piper *(1903–92, UK)*

After working at his father's law office until 1927, Piper studied at Richmond School of Art and the Royal College of Art, London. From 1940 to 1942 he was an official war artist. Piper is best known for his paintings and stained glass, but he also designed books, textiles, and ceramics.

"Chiesa Della Salute" fabric, c.1965

Giancarlo Piretti *(b. 1940, Italy)*

After graduating from the State Art Institute of Bologna in 1960, Piretti began designing furniture for Anonima Castelli, where he first used plastic for the award-winning "Plia" folding chair (1969). In the late 1970s, he started developing office furniture with Emilio Ambasz, including the adjustable "Vertebra" armchair (1974–7).

"Plia" folding chairs, 1969

Warren Platner *(1919–2006, USA)*

Platner studied architecture at Cornell University, graduating in 1941. From 1945 to 1950, he worked for Raymond Loewy and I.M. Pei, and for Eero Saarinen from 1960 to 1965. He is best known for the collection of wire-framed furniture he created for Knoll.

A Knoll lounge chair, 1966

Flavio Poli *(1900–84, Italy)*

After training in ceramics, Poli became a glass sculptor for I.V.A.M. on Murano in 1929. He joined the Seguso-Barovier-Ferro glassworks (known as Seguso Vetri d'Arte from 1937) in 1934, where he was artistic director until 1963. In the 1950s, he made colourful cased-glass vases.

A Seguso Vetri d'Arte sommerso glass vase, c.1965

Gio Ponti *(1891–1979, Italy)*

A 1930s dining table

Gio Ponti studied architecture at Milan's Polytechnic Institute, graduating in 1921. In 1928, he launched the design journal *Domus*, and during his remarkable career, Ponti designed buildings, ceramics, furniture, metalware, and glass. He is best known for his ceramics for Richard Ginori, the furniture he designed with Piero Fornasetti, and the "Superleggera" chair (1957) for Cassina.

Harvey Probber *(1922–2003, USA)*

A pair of low-back chairs

While still at high school, Probber commuted to Manhattan to sell his sketches to furniture manufacturers. He took evening classes in design at the Pratt Institute while learning furniture production by day at New York company Trade Upholstery. His furniture is characterized by modern lines with warm details, such as bright colours.

Phillip Lloyd Powell *(1919–2008, USA)*

A walnut dining table

Powell studied engineering at the Drexel Institute of Technology in Philadelphia, and moved to New Hope, Pennsylvania, after World War II. After building his own house, he was urged by his neighbour, George Nakashima, to design furniture. He established a showroom in 1953, which he shared with Paul Evans from 1956.

Jean Prouvé *(1901–84, France)*

A 'Standard' Chair, c.1930

After serving his apprenticeship as an art metalworker, Prouvé opened his own workshop in Nancy in 1923. He began designing metal furniture in 1924, and won commissions from Le Corbusier. He founded a large factory, Les Ateliers Jean Prouvé, in 1947 but resigned in 1953. From 1954, he worked at his design studio in Paris.

Emilio Pucci *(1914–92, Italy)*

Pucci's designs first received attention in 1947 after a skiing outfit of his was photographed by *Harper's Bazaar*. The resulting success encouraged him to open his own *haute couture* house. He designed the first of the bright, geometric prints he is now known for in 1962.

David Queensberry *(b. 1929, UK)*

Trained at London's Central School of Arts and Crafts, Queensberry was an apprentice at a ceramics manufacturer in Stoke-on-Trent in 1953. He designed popular wares for Crown Staffordshire and Midwinter, and was Professor of Ceramics at the Royal College of Art, London, from 1959 to 1983. In 1966, he set up Queensberry Hunt with fellow ceramics designer Martin Hunt.

Jens Quistgaard *(1919–2008, Denmark)*

As well as training as a silversmith with Georg Jensen, Quistgaard studied sculpture, carpentry, and ceramics. After World War II, he started producing product designs in the Danish Modern Style, and in 1954 set up a company, Dansk Design, to manufacture his cookware, cutlery, and elegant teak vessels.

Ernest Race *(1913–64, UK)*

After studying interior design at the Bartlett School of Architecture, London, from 1932 to 1935, race worked for a lighting company, where he met Modernist luminaries such as Walter Gropius. In 1937 he started selling textiles woven in India to his designs, and in 1945 he co-founded Ernest Race Ltd to mass-produce Utility furniture, such as his highly successful "BA" chair (1945).

Dieter Rams (b. 1932, Germany)

Rams studied architecture and interior design at the Crafts Art School in Wiesbaden, taking three years out to gain practical experience in a carpentry workshop. He graduated in 1953. From 1955 he worked for Braun, becoming head of the design department in 1961, and director of design in 1968. During the 1960s he also designed furniture for Vitsoe.

T. H. Robsjohn-Gibbings

(1905–76, UK/USA)

Robsjohn-Gibbings studied architecture at London University before moving to the USA in 1930. In 1936 he opened a showroom on Madison Avenue, New York, displaying Classical-inspired furniture of his own design. In 1948 he became chief designer of the Widdicomb furniture company. In 1966, he moved to Greece.

Jens Risom (b. 1916, Denmark/USA)

Risom studied furniture and interior design at the School of Arts and Crafts in Copenhagen from 1935 to 1938. He moved to the USA in 1939, where he started out by designing textiles for Dan Cooper in New York. In 1941, he designed the first chair produced by Knoll. He freelanced for Georg Jensen (among others) between 1941 and 1943, and established Jens Risom Design in 1946.

Sérgio Rodrigues (b. 1927, Brazil)

Rodrigues studied at the National School of Architecture, in Rio de Janeiro, graduating in 1952. After running a modern art and furniture store, he founded a furniture company, Oca, in 1955. He left the company in 1968 to design independently. He typically uses natural, local materials, such as leather, wood, and rattan. He is best known for his "Sheriff" chair (1957).

René Roubicek (b. 1922, Czech Republic)

Roubicek studied at the Academy of Applied Arts, Prague, graduating in 1950. He taught at Kamenický Šenov glass school from 1945 to 1952, and went on to design for Crystalex in Nový Bor until 1965, before returning to teach in Prague from 1966 to 1968. He became an independent glass artist in 1966.

Lino Sabattini (b. 1925, Italy)

Largely self-taught, Sabattini set up his own metalworking studio in Milan in 1955. From 1956 to 1963, he produced sleek and abstract designs for French company Christofle. He set up a studio, Argenteria Sabattini, in 1964 to produce his designs.

Eero Saarinen (1910–61, Finland/USA)

The son of architect Eliel Saarinen, Eero Saarinen moved to the USA with his family in 1923. He studied sculpture in Paris from 1929 to 1930, and architecture at Yale, graduating in 1934. After early collaborations with Charles Eames, he began creating organically shaped furniture for Knoll. He opened Eero Saarinen & Associates in 1950. a small scale. He also designed glass and ceramics.

Richard Sapper (b. 1932, Germany)

Sapper studied mechanical engineering and economics in Munich, graduating in 1954. He moved to Milan in 1957 to work for Gio Ponti. He worked for Marco Zanuso from 1959 to 1961, and continued to collaborate with him until 1977. Sapper opened his own design office in Stuttgart in 1970. Best known for his industrial products, he has also designed furniture for Knoll, Molteni, and Castelli.

Gino Sarfatti *(1912–84, Italy)*

Arteluce floor lamps, 1956

Sarfatti studied aeronaval engineering at the University of Genoa. He founded the lighting company, Arteluce, in 1939, and designed many of its products. He also designed lighting for Arredoluce. His designs are typically sleek, often featuring coloured shades.

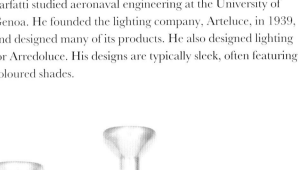

Timo Sarpaneva *(1926–2006, Finland)*

An Iittala "Lancet II" glass form, 1952

Sarpaneva studied graphic design at the University of Art and Design, Helsinki, from 1941 to 1948. He joined Iittala in 1950 and soon began developing new glass manufacturing techniques. In the mid 1950s he taught at the College of Applied Arts, Helsinki, and was awarded a Grand Prix at the 1951 and 1957 Milan Triennales.

Raymond Savignac *(1907–2002, France)*

In 1924, Savignac was hired by the advertising agency Lortac, where he assisted A. M. Cassandre. In the 1930s, he began producing his own posters. Often humorous, they were based on a sole graphic element: "A single image for a single idea." The "Monsavon" poster (1949) is one of his best known designs.

Carlo Scarpa *(1906–78, Italy)*

A Venini "Tessuto" glass vase, c.1940

Scarpa studied architecture in Venice, graduating in 1926 and founding his own architectural practice in 1927. From 1926 to 1930, he was design consultant to the Murano glassworks M. V. M. Cappellin. From 1932 to 1947, he worked with Venini, where he introduced the *sommerso* glass technique. He also designed furniture for Gavina.

Tobia Scarpa *(b. 1935-, Italy)*

The son of Carlo Scarpa, Tobia Scarpa studied architecture in Venice. From 1957 to 1961, he designed glass for Venini. He set up a design office with his wife, Afra, in 1960. They designed furniture for companies such as Gavinia, B&B Italia, Knoll, and Molteni, as well as lighting, flatware, interiors and corporate identities.

Peter *(1923–2003, UK)*
and Alison Smithson *(1928–93, UK)*

The Smithsons studied architecture in Durham from 1944 to 1949, and moved to London in 1950. They are best known for their New Brutalist architecture and influential ideas on housing and town planning, but also designed several important pieces of furniture, including the "Trundling Turk" chair (1954).

Hans Schleger *(1898–1976, Germany)*

Schleger (also known as Zéró) studied at the National School of Applied Art, Berlin, from 1918 to 1921. He moved to New York in 1924, back to Berlin in 1929, and to the UK in 1939. During World War II, Schleger designed many innovative posters for London Transport, the Ministry of Food, and the General Post Office.

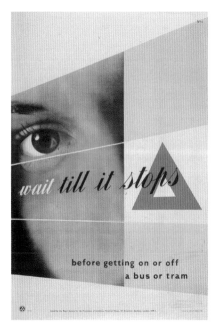

Ettore Sottsass *(1917–2007, Austria/Italy)*

Sottsass studied architecture in Turin from 1935 to 1939. He became artistic director of Poltronova in 1957, and was a design consultant for Olivetti from 1958. His designs are always colourful and innovative, and he is best known for the Postmodern furniture he produced for the Memphis group, which he co-founded in 1981.

William Spratling (1900–67, USA/Mexico)

Spratling studied architecture at the Alabama Polytechnic Institute. In 1921 he became Associate Professor of Architecture at Tulane University, New Orleans. In 1929 he moved to Taxco, Mexico, which had silver mines, but no local silverworking industry. Spratling designed silverware based on pre-Columbian and traditional motifs, and hired local goldsmiths to produce them.

Ronald Stennett-Wilson (1915–2010, UK)

Stennett-Wilson began designing glass when he was sales manager of J. Wuidart & Co, an importer of Scandinavian wares. The glass was made in Scandinavia and sold through Wuidart. He founded King's Lynn Glass in 1967, and Langham Glass in 1979. He also wrote influential books, including *The Beauty of Modern Glass* (1975).

Irene Stevens (b. 1917, UK)

Stevens studied at the Royal College of Art, London. She began working for Webb Corbett in 1946 as chief designer, producing bold, modern designs that shaped the company's output. She left in 1957 to join the faculty of the glass department at Stourbridge College.

Nanny Still *(1926–2009. Finland)*

Having attracted the attention of Riihimäki glassworks in 1949 while still a student at Helsinki's Institute of Applied Art, Still produced designs for the company from 1949 to 1976, gaining international renown for her "Harlekini" series (1958). She also designed ceramics, jewellery, graphics, and metalware.

Josef Švarc *(b. 1928. Czech Republic)*

Švarc studied at the Kamenický Šenov glass school from 1949 to 1952, and the School of Applied Art in Brno from 1952 to 1954. He worked briefly for Nový Bor, then for the Bohemia glassworks at Svetlá and Sázavou from 1953 to 1973, and for Josefodol. He is known for his cut and engraved glass, particularly with designs from nature.

Jiri Šuhájek *(b. 1943. Czech Republic)*

Šuhájek studied at the glass school at Kamenický Šenov from 1957 to 1961, at the Academy of Applied Art in Prague under Stanislav Libenský from 1964 to 1968, and at the Royal College of Art, London from 1968 to 1971. He designed for Moser from 1972 to 1978, and later for the Institute of Interior and Fashion Design in Prague.

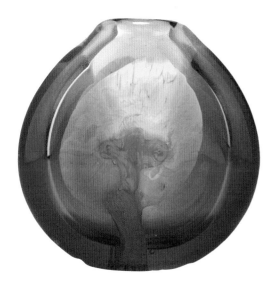

Jessie Tait *(1928–2010. UK)*

Tait studied at the Burslem School of Art in Stoke-on-Trent from the age of 13 to 18. In 1946, following a brief apprenticeship to Charlotte Rhead, she joined Midwinter. She worked at Johnson Brothers, a division of Wedgwood, from 1974 to 1993. She later become a freelance designer.

Kazuhide Takahama *(b. 1930, Japan)*

Takahama studied architecture at the Tokyo Institute of Technology, graduating in 1953. In 1957, he began designing furniture and lighting for Gavina, including the modular "Dadà" storage unit (1965). His designs are typically stark and modern, but with a Japanese appreciation for natural materials and aesthetics.

Joaquim Tenreiro *(1906–92, Portugal/Brazil)*

Born into a family of Portuguese furniture-makers, Tenreiro moved to Brazil in 1928. He worked for furniture makers including Leandro Martins, Francisco Gomes, and Laubisch & Hirt, before founding his own furniture studio, Langenbach & Tenreiro, in the early 1940s. His designs are typically light and elegant.

Ilmari Tapiovaara *(1914–99, Finland)*

Tapiovaara studied interior design, graduating in 1937. Having worked for Asko in 1938, he became the artistic and commercial director of the Keravan Puuteollisuus furniture company in 1941. He established his own office with his wife in 1951. Tapiovaara's designs are strongly influenced by Alvar Aalto. His best-known creation is the "Domus" chair (1946–7).

Nils Thorsson *(1898–1975, Sweden/Denmark)*

Aged 13, Thorsson was apprenticed to the Aluminia Factory (part of Royal Copenhagen), and graduated from the Royal Danish Academy in 1917. He became one of Royal Copenhagen's most prolific designers, and was artistic director from 1928 to 1969. His best-known ranges include "Solbjerg" (1934) and "Marselis" (1953).

Frank Thrower (1932–87, UK)

A Dartington decanter

Thrower became sales director of Portmeirion Pottery, Wales, in 1960, and while there, he designed his first glassware. He established Dartington glassworks with Peter Sutcliffe in 1967. Thrower designed more than 500 pieces of mostly mould-blown glass for the company.

Helena Tynell (b. 1918, Finland)

A Riihimaen Lasi Oy "Aurinkopullo" (sun bottle), 1964

Tynell trained as a sculptor in Helsinki, graduating in 1943. She joined Riihimäki in 1946, and began to produce large, bold, colourful mould-blown designs from 1961. She left in 1976, and designed lamps for Bega-Limburg before returning to studio glassmaking in 1993.

Ermanno Toso (1903–73, Italy)

A Fratelli Toso, "Murrine" vase, c.1960

Toso joined the Fratelli Toso glassworks on Murano in 1924, and became marketing and artistic director of the company in 1936. Toso pioneered the company's new Modern style, designing many important pieces using updated techniques, such as the use of murrines.

Henry Varnum Poor (1887–1970, USA)

A faience charger, 1947

Poor studied painting at London's Slade School and in Paris. He began making hand-thrown ceramics in the 1920s. In 1946 he co-founded the Skowhegan School of Painting and Sculpture. Known for his paintings, murals, and ceramics, he was also an architect and writer.

Victor Vasarely (1906–97, Hungary/France)

After studying medicine in Budapest, in the late 1920s Vasarely trained as a painter and graphic artist. In 1930 he moved to Paris. He developed his optical art style in the 1940s and 1950s. In the 1970s, he designed for Rosenthal.

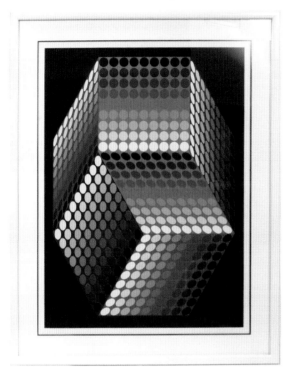

Massimo Vignelli (b. 1931, Italy)

Vignelli studied architecture in Milan in the early 1950s. He ran a design and architecture studio with his wife Lella in Milan from 1960. In 1965 they moved to the USA, and set up Vignelli Associates in New York in 1971. Vignelli is known for corporate identities, furniture, and glass. Typical designs feature clean lines and block colours.

Paolo Venini (1895–1959, Italy)

Originally trained as a lawyer, Venini set up his first glassworks with Giacomo Cappellin in 1921, and his own firm in 1925. His innovations of the late 1920s include *vetro pulegoso* (bubbled glass). In the 1950s and 1960s, Venini produced many notable designs by key designers.

František Vízner (1936–2011, Czech Republic)

Vízner studied at the Železný Brod glass school from 1953 to 1956, and the Academy of Applied Art in Prague from 1952 to 1962. He designed pressed glass for Sklo Union from 1962 to 1967, and then the Arts & Crafts Centre at Skrdlovice until 1977. He is best known for the large cut and polished studio glass pieces he made after 1977.

Arne Vodder (1926–2009. Denmark)

Vodder was trained by Finn Juhl, whom he later collaborated with. In 1951 he set up a studio with architect Anton Borg. His furniture designs were produced by companies such a Fritz Hansen, France & Son/Cado and, most notably, Sibast. His preferred materials were rosewood and teak.

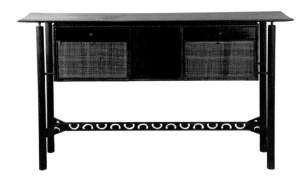

Wilhelm Wagenfeld (1900–90. Germany)

After an apprenticeship at a silverware company, Wagefeld studied in Bremen and Hanau from 1914 to 1922 before training in metalwork under Lásló Moholy-Nagy at the Bauhaus. Best known for his "MT8" lamp (1923–4), he also designed glassware for Schott and ceramics for Fürstenberg and Rosenthal.

Ole Wanscher (1903–85. Denmark)

Wanscher graduated from the Danish School of Art and Design in 1924. He worked with his former tutor, Kaare Klint, until 1927, and set up his own office in 1928. He worked for P. Jeppesen Møbelfabrik in the 1950s. His pieces were inspired by sources ranging from 18th-century British furniture to Egyptian and Chinese design.

Andy Warhol (1928–87. USA)

Warhol studied commercial art at the Carnegie Institute of Technology, Pittsburgh. He moved to New York in 1949 and began working in advertising. His first solo exhibition took place in 1962. He was known for his Pop Art style and, as well as making paintings and prints, Warhol also produced sculptures, films, and music. He is considered to be a major artist of the twentieth-century.

Hans Wegner (1914–2007. Denmark)

After serving a carpentry apprenticeship, Wegner studied at the Copenhagen Institute of Technology from, 1936 to 1938, and later at the city's School of Arts and Crafts. From 1940 he worked with Erik Møller and Arne Jacobsen, establishing his own studio in 1946. He is best known for his solid wood chairs, which were manufactured by companies such as Fritz Hansen.

Robert Welch *(1929–2000, UK)*

Milk and coffee pots, 1957

Welch studied silversmithing at Birmingham School of Art, and at the Royal College of Art, London. In 1955 he set up a studio in Gloucestershire, and from 1955 to 1984 he worked as design consultant for J. & J. Wiggin/Old Hall, winning three Design Council awards for his work.

Bjørn Wiinblad *(1918–2006 Denmark)*

A Nymølle wall candle sconce

Wiinblad studied at the Danish Royal Academy of Fine Arts, Copenhagen, and set up his own studio in 1952. He began working Nymølle in 1946, taking over the company in 1976, and also designed for Rosenthal from 1956. Wiinblad is best known for whimsical ceramics, but he also designed glass, silver, furniture, posters, and textiles.

William Wilson *(1905–72, UK)*

A Whitefriars "Molar" vase, c.1955

In the 1930s and 1940s, Wilson designed coloured glass for Whitefriars. He became head designer and managing director in 1948, hiring Geoffrey Baxter in 1954. In 1964 he introduced the "Knobbly" range for Whitefriars, which represented the company's first step towards textured glass.

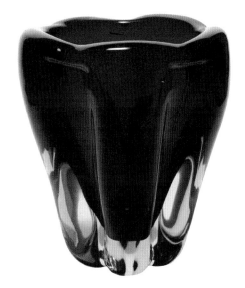

Tapio Wirkkala *(1915–85. Finland)*

Wirkkala studied sculpture at the University of Art and Design, Helsinki, from 1933 to 1936. He designed for Iittala from 1946, with his "Kantarelli" vase (1946) helping to establish his international reputation. He worked in Raymond Loewy's office from 1955 to 1956. Apart from glass, he also designed furniture, ceramics, metalware, and lighting.

Edward Wormley (1907–95, USA)

Wormley enrolled at the Art Institute of Chicago in 1926, but was forced to drop out in 1928. He worked in the design studio of department store Marshall Field's from 1928 to 1930. In 1931, he began designing traditional and modern-style furniture for Dunbar. In 1945, he opened his own office, but continued as a consultant at Dunbar.

Russel Wright (1904–76, USA)

Wright studied painting in Cincinnati and sculpture at the Art Students League of New York. He designed theatre sets before producing a range of spun aluminium bar accessories, and set up his own workshop in 1930. He is best known for the "American Modern" dinnerware (1937) he designed for Steubenville Pottery.

Karel Wunsch (b. 1932, Czech Republic)

Wunsch studied at the glass school in Nový Bor from 1946 to 1950, and at the Academy of Applied Art in Prague under Josef Kaplický from 1953 to 1959. He worked at the Nový Bor glassworks from 1959 to 1969, designing engraved, cut, or painted vessels. Wunsch also designed tableware and architectural glass.

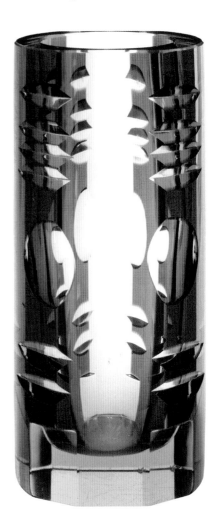

Sori Yanagi (1915–2011, Japan)

After studying painting and architecture at the Tokyo School of Fine Arts, Yanagi worked in Charlotte Perriand's Tokyo office from 1940 to 1942. In 1952, he founded the Yanagi Industrial Design Institute. He is known for combining traditional Japanese craftsmanship and new techniques in designs such as the "Butterfly" stool (1954).

Vladimir Zahour (b. 1925, Czech Republic)

A 1960s–70s Podebrady ashtray

Zahour studied at the glass school at Železný Brod from 1939 to 1943, and at the Academy of Applied Art in Prague from 1944 to 1950. He joined the Bohemia glassworks in Podebrady as a manager and designer in 1953. He is best known for his pressed glass and cut lead crystal designs.

Eva Zeisel (1906–2011, Hungary)

A late 1930s Hallcraft soup dish with "Fantasy" pattern

After originally studying painting, Zeisel started designing ceramics in the late 1920s for German companies such as Majolika-Fabrik Schramberg. She lived and worked in Russia in the mid 1930s. In 1938, she moved to New York. With ranges such as "Museum" (1946) and "Town and Country" (1946–7), she brought practical, sculptural modern ceramics into middle-class American homes.

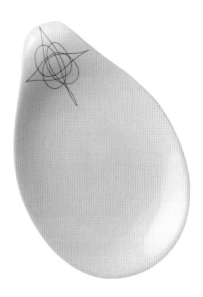

Marco Zanuso (1916–2001, Italy)

A "Marcuso" table, 1960

Zanuso studied architecture at Milan's Polytechnic Institute, graduating in 1939. He founded a design and architecture office in Milan in 1945. In 1949 he designed the latex foam "Antropus" chair for Pirelli's manufacturing company Arflex. From 1958 to 1977, he collaborated on product designs with Richard Sapper.

František Zemek (1913–60, Czech Republic)

A Mstisov glassworks "Harmony" range vase

After working as a cutter at the Dobronin glassworks, Zemek studied at the Železný Brod glass school from 1938 to 1940, and at the Academy of Applied Art in Prague until 1948. In the 1950s, he worked at the Kamenický Šenov and Železný Brod glassworks, became head designer at Mstivov, and also designed for Moser.

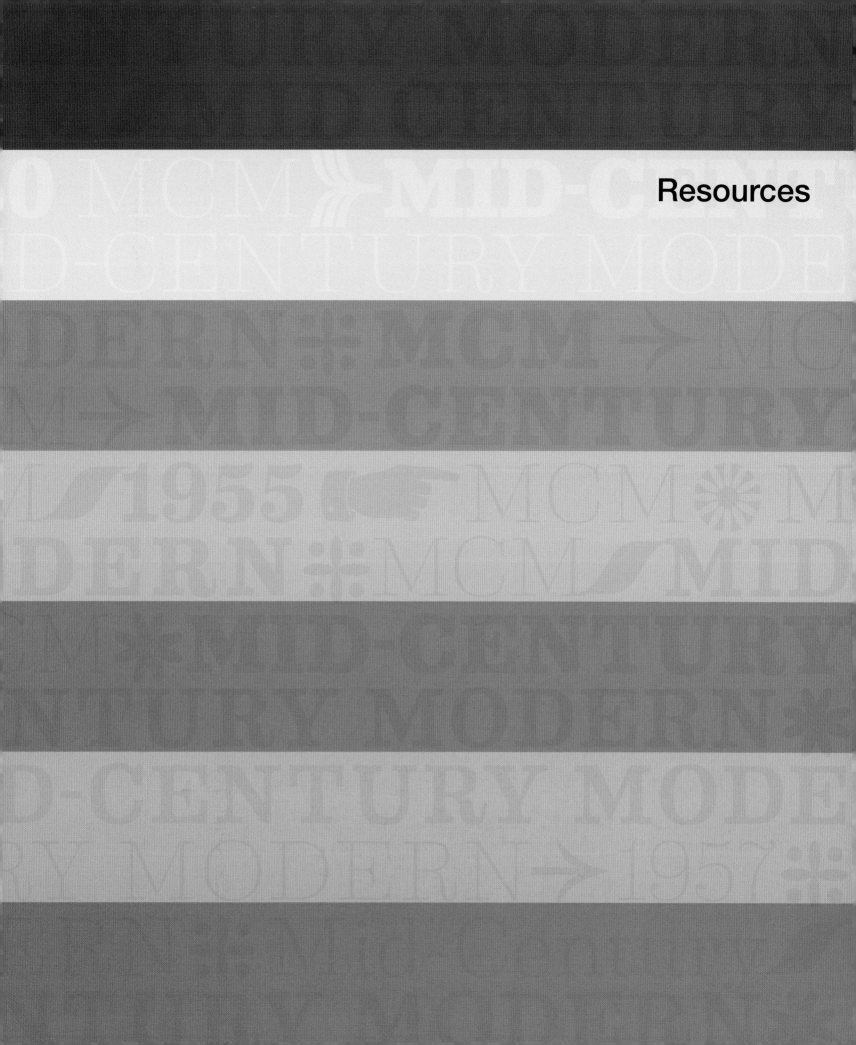

Resources

Ceramics

Beth Adams
Stand GO23-25/28-30
Alfies Antiques Market
13-25 Church Street
Marylebone
London NW8 8DT
Tel: +44 7776 136 003
www.alfiesantiques.com

The End of History
548 1/2 Hudson Street,
New York, NY 10014, USA
Tel: +1 212 647 7598
historyglass@gmail.com
www.theendofhistoryshop.blogspot.com

Fragile Design
14-15 The Custard Factory, Digbeth,
Birmingham, B9 4AA, England
Tel: +44 121 224 7378 or 07766 770 920
info@fragiledesign.com
www.fragiledesign.com

Hi & Lo Modern
artsponge@gmail.com
www.hiandlomodern.com

Quittenbaum
Theresienstrasse 60,
D-80333 Munich, Germany
Tel: +49 89 2737021-25
www.quittenbaum.de

Rago Arts
333 North Main Street,
Lambertville,
NJ 08530, USA
Tel: +1 609 397 9374
info@ragoarts.com
www.ragoarts.com

Retroselect
info@retroselect.com
www.retroselect.com

Geoffrey Robinson
Alfies Antiques Market,
Stands GO77/78 & GO91/92,
13-25 Church Street,
London, NW8 8DT,
England

Tel: +44 7794 085 723
www.robinsonantiques.co.uk
(Submit written enquiries through the website)

Undercurrents
28 Cowper Street,
London, EC2A 4AS,
England
Tel: +44 207251 1537
shop@undercurrents.biz
www.undercurrents.biz

Richard Wallis Antiks
Tel: +44 208523 8127 or
+44 7721 583 306
info@richardwallisantiks.co.uk
www.richardwallisantiks.com

Skinner
63 Park Plaza, Boston,
MA012116, USA
www.skinnerinc.com

Von Zezschwitz
Friedrichstrasse 1a,
80801 Munich, Germany
Tel: +49 89 38 98 930
www.von-zezschwitz.de

Woolley & Wallis
51-61 Castle Street,
Salisbury, SP1 3SU, England
Tel: +44 1722 424 500
enquiries@woolleyandwallis.co.uk
www.woolleyandwallis.co.uk

Homewares

Ian Broughton
Alfie's Antiques Market,
Stands S48/49 & 59/60,
13-25 Church Street,
London, NW8 8DT, England
Tel: +44 207723 6066
ianbroughton@hotmail.com
www.alfiesantiques.com

Fragile Design
14-15 The Custard Factory,
Digbeth, Birmingham B9 4AA
Tel: +44 121 224 7378 or
+44 7766 770 920
info@fragiledesign.com
www.fragiledesign.com

Furniture

20th Century Marks
Oak Lodge, Rectory Road,
Little Burstead,
Essex, CM12 9TR, England
Tel: +44 474 872 460
www.20thcenturymarks.co.uk

20th Century Provenance
31 Exchange Street, Pawtucket,
Rhode Island 02860, USA
info@provenance20.com
www.provenance20.com

Atomic Antiques
125 Shoreditch High Street,
London, E1 6JE, England
Tel: +44 207739 5923
email@atomica.me.uk
www.atomica.me.uk

Boomerang for Modern
2475 Kettner Blvd
San Diego, CA 92101 USA
Tel: +1 619 239 2040
david@boomerangsd.com
www.boomerangformodern.com

Eames Office
850 Pico Boulevard
Santa Monica, CA 90405, USA
Tel: +1 310 369 5991
info@eamesoffice.com
www.eamesoffice.com

Fragile Design
14-15 The Custard Factory,
Digbeth, Birmingham, B9 4AA, England
Tel: +44 121 224 7378 or
+44 7766 770 920
info@fragiledesign.com
www.fragiledesign.com

Herman Miller
www.hermanmiller.com

Knoll
www.knoll.com

The Modern Warehouse
3 Trafalgar Mews,
Hackney, London E9 5JG
Tel: +44 208986 0740 or

David: +44 7747 758 852
Rob: +44 7930 304 361
info@themodernwarehouse.com
www.themodernwarehouse.com
Origin Modernism
Tel: +44 20 8469 0945
info@originmodernism.co.uk
www.originmodernism.co.uk

Planet Bazaar
Arch 68, The Stables Market,
Chalk Farm Road,
London NW1 8AH
Tel: +44 207485 6000
www.planetbazaar.co.uk

Quittenbaum
Theresienstrasse 60,
D-80333 Munich, Germany
Tel: +49 89 2737021-25
www.quittenbaum.de

Rago Arts
333 North Main Street,
Lambertville, NJ 08530, USA
Tel: 609 397 9374
info@ragoarts.com
www.ragoarts.com

R 20th Century Design
82 Franklin Street,
New York, NY 10013, USA
www.20thcentury.com

Skinner
63 Park Plaza, Boston,
MA012116, USA
www.skinnerinc.com

TwentyTwentyOne
18c River Street
London EC1R 1XN
Tel: +44 207837 1900
mail@twentytwentyone.com
www.twentytwentyone.com

Vitra Ltd.
www.vitra.com

Von Zezschwitz
Friedrichstrasse 1a,
80801 Munich, Germany
Tel: 0049 89 38 98 930
www.von-zezschwitz.de

Woolley & Wallis
51-61 Castle Street,
Salisbury SP1 3SU
Tel: +44 1722 424 500
enquiries@woolleyandwallis.co.uk
www.woolleyandwallis.co.uk

Glass

Nigel Benson
20th Century Glass
Tel: +44 7971 859 848
nigelbenson@20thcentury-glass.com
www.20thcentury-glass.com

Jeanette Hayhurst Glass
Long Street Antiques
14 Long Street
Tetbury
GL8 8AQ
Tel: +44 7831 209 814
www.antiqueglass-london.com

Cynthia Findlay
Toronto Antiques on King
284 King Street West,
Toronto, Ontario M5V 1J2
Tel: 416.260.9057
askcynthia@cynthiafindlay.com
www.torontoantiquesonking.com

Dr. Fischer
Trappensee-Schlösschen
74074 Heilbronn, Germany
Tel: 0049 7131 15557 0
info@auctions-fischer.de
www.auctions-fischer.de

Fragile Design
14-15 The Custard Factory, Digbeth,
Birmingham B9 4AA
Tel: +44 121 224 7378 or
+44 7766 770 920
info@fragiledesign.com
www.fragiledesign.com

Glass etc
18-22 Rope Walk, Rye,
East Sussex TN31 7NA
Tel: +44 1797 226 600
andy@decanterman.com
www.decanterman.com

Hi & Lo Modern
artsponge@gmail.com
www.hiandlomodern.com

Francesca Martire
First Floor, Alfies Antiques Market,
13-25 Church Street,
London NW8 8DT
Tel: +44 7724 4802
info@francescamartire.com
www.francescamartire.com

Pips Trip
13 Pyne Road,
Surbiton,
Surrey KT6 7BN
sales@pips-trip.co.uk
www.pips-trip.co.uk

Planet Bazaar
Arch 68, The Stables Market, Chalk Farm
Road, London NW1 8AH
Tel: +44 207485 6000
info@planetbazaar.co.uk
www.planetbazaar.co.uk

Quittenbaum
Theresienstrasse 60,
D-80333 Munich, Germany
Tel: 0049 89 2737021-25
www.quittenbaum.de

Retro Art Glass
Murrieta, California
Tel: 951.639.3032
retroartglass@verizon.net
www.retroartglass.com

Retropolitan
Tel: +44 7870 422 182
enquiries@retropolitan.co.uk
www.retropolitan.co.uk

The Studio Glass Merchant
info@thestudioglassmerchant.co.uk
www.thestudioglassmerchant.co.uk

Von Zezschwitz
Friedrichstrasse 1a,
80801 Munich, Germany
Tel: 0049 89 38 98 930
www.von-zezschwitz.de
Woolley & Wallis
51-61 Castle Street,
Salisbury SP1 3SU
Tel: +44 1722 424 500
enquiries@woolleyandwallis.co.uk

Lighting

20th Century Marks
Oak Lodge, Rectory Road,
Little Burstead,
Essex CM12 9TR
Tel: +44 1474 872 460
michael@20thcenturymarks.co.uk
adam@20thcenturymarks.co.uk
www.20thcenturymarks.co.uk

20th Century Provenance
31 Exchange Street
Pawtucket
Rhode Island 02860 USA
www.provenance20.com

Atomic Antiques
125 Shoreditch High Street
London E1 6JE
Tel: +44 207739 5923
email@atomica.me.uk
www.atomica.me.uk

Chameleon Fine Lighting
223 East 59th Street,
New York, NY 10022
Tel: 212 355 6300
mail@chameleon59.com
www.chameleon59.com

Francesca Martire
First Floor,
Alfies Antiques Market,
13-25 Church Street,
London NW8 8DT
Tel: +44 207724 4802
www.francescamartire.com

The Modern Warehouse
3 Trafalgar Mews,
Hackney, London E9 5JG
Tel: +44 208986 0740 or
David: +44 7747 758 852
Rob: +44 7930 304 361
www.themodernwarehouse.com

Planet Bazaar
Arch 68, The Stables Market,
Chalk Farm Road,
London NW1 8AH
Tel: +44 207485 6000
info@planetbazaar.co.uk
www.planetbazaar.co.uk

Quittenbaum
Theresienstrasse 60,
D-80333 Munich, Germany
Tel: 0049 89 2737021-25
www.quittenbaum.de

20th Century Design
82 Franklin Street, New York,
NY 10013, USA
www.20thcentury.com

TwentyTwentyOne
18c River Street
London EC1R 1XN
Tel: +44 207837 1900
mail@twentytwentyone.com
www.twentytwentyone.com

Von Zezschwitz
Friedrichstrasse 1a,
80801 Munich, Germany
Tel: 0049 89 38 98 930
www.von-zezschwitz.de

Woolley & Wallis
51-61 Castle Street,
Salisbury SP1 3SU
Tel: +44 1722 424 500
enquiries@woolleyandwallis.co.uk
www.woolleyandwallis.co.uk

Metalware

Cynthia Findlay
Toronto Antiques on King
284 King Street West,
Toronto, Ontario M5V 1J2
Tel: +1 416 260 9057
askcynthia@cynthiafindlay.com
www.torontoantiquesonking.com

The End of History
548 1/2 Hudson Street,
New York, NY 10014
Tel: +1 212 647 7598
historyglass@gmail.com
www.theendofhistoryshop.blogspot.com

Hi & Lo Modern
artsponge@gmail.com
www.hiandlomodern.com

Georg Jensen
Stores located internationally
www.georgjensen.com
The London Silver Vaults
Chancery Lane, London
WC2A 1QS
www.thesilvervaults.com

Quittenbaum
Theresienstrasse 60,
D-80333 Munich, Germany
Tel: +49 89 2737021-25
www.quittenbaum.de

Rago Arts
333 North Main Street,
Lambertville, NJ 08530
Tel: +609 397 9374
info@ragoarts.com
www.ragoarts.com

Geoffrey Robinson
Alfies Antiques Market,
Stands GO77/78 & GO91/92,
13-25 Church Street,
London NW8 8DT
Tel: +44 7794 085 723
www.robinsonantiques.co.uk
(Submit enquiries through the website)

Von Zezschwitz
Friedrichstrasse 1a,
80801 Munich, Germany
Tel: +49 89 38 98 930
www.von-zezschwitz.de

Woolley & Wallis
51-61 Castle Street,
Salisbury SP1 3SU
Tel: +44 1722 424 500
enquiries@woolleyandwallis.co.uk
www.woolleyandwallis.co.uk

Textiles

Fragile Design
14-15 The Custard Factory, Digbeth,
Birmingham, B9 4AA, England
Tel: +44 121 224 7378 or
+44 7766 770 920
info@fragiledesign.com
www.fragiledesign.com

Hi & Lo Modern
artsponge@gmail.com
www.hiandlomodern.com
Leslie Hindman Auctioneers
1338 West Lake Street, Chicago,
IL 60607, USA
Tel: +1 312 280 1212
www.lesliehindman.com

Quittenbaum
Theresienstrasse 60,
D-80333 Munich, Germany
Tel: +49 89 2737021 25
www.quittenbaum.de

Rago Arts
333 North Main Street,
Lambertville, NJ 08530, USA
Tel: +1 609 397 9374
info@ragoarts.com
www.ragoarts.com

Kerry Taylor Auctions
Unit C21, Parkhall Road Trading Estate,
40 Martell Road, London, SE21 8EN, England
Tel: +44 208676 4600
info@kerrytaylorauctions.com
www.kerrytaylorauctions.com

Von Zezschwitz
Friedrichstrasse 1a,
80801 Munich, Germany
Tel: +49 89 38 98 930
www.von-zezschwitz.de

Woolley & Wallis
51-61 Castle Street,
Salisbury, SP1 3SU, England
Tel: +44 1722 424 500
enquiries@woolleyandwallis.co.uk
www.woolleyandwallis.co.uk

Antiques fairs and shows
UK:
Antiques for Everyone
www.antiquesforeveryone.co.uk

Modern Shows
www.modernshows.com

Nelson Events
www.nelsonevents.co.uk

Olympia International Fine Art & Antiques Fair
www.olympia-art-antiques.com

USA:
Alameda Point Antiques Faire
alamedapointantiquesfaire.com
Brimfield Antiques and Collectibles Show
www.brimfieldshow.com

Brooklyn Flea Market
www.brooklynflea.com

The Farm Chicks
www.thefarmchicks.com

Sandwich Antiques Market
www.antiquemarkets.com

Museums:
UK:
Design Museum
28 Shad Thames, London, SE1 2YD
www.designmuseum.org

Geffrye Museum
Kingsland Road, London, E2 8EA
www.geffrye-museum.org.uk

Manchester Art Gallery
Mosley Street, Manchester, M2 3JL
www.manchestergalleries.org

National Glass Centre
Liberty Way, Sunderland, SR6 0GL
www.nationalglasscentre.com
Victoria & Albert Museum
Cromwell Road, London SW7 2RL
www.vam.ac.uk

The Whitworth Art Gallery
The University of Manchester,
Oxford Road, Manchester, M15 6ER
www.whitworth.manchester.ac.uk

Europe:
Alvar Aalto Museum
Alvar Aallon katu 7,
Jyväskylä, Finland
www.alvaraalto.fi

Design Museum
Korkeavuorenkatu 23 00130
Helsinki, Finland
www.designmuseum.fi
Designmuseum Danmark
Bredgade 68/1260 København
www.designmuseum.dk

Vitra Design Museum
Charles-Eames-Str. 2, D-79576
Weil am Rhein, Germany
www.design-museum.de

USA:
The Chicago Athenaeum Museum
of Architecture and Design
The Historic Fulton Brewery Building,
601 South Prospect Street, Galena,
IL 61036
www.chi-athenaeum.org

Cooper Hewitt National Design Museum
2 East 91st St, New York,
NY 10128
www.cooperhewitt.org

The Metropolitan Museum of Art
1000 Fifth Avenue, New York,
NY 10028-0198
www.metmuseum.org

The Museum of Modern Art
11 West 53 Street, New York, NY 10019
www.moma.org

Magazines
www.midcenturymagazine.co.uk

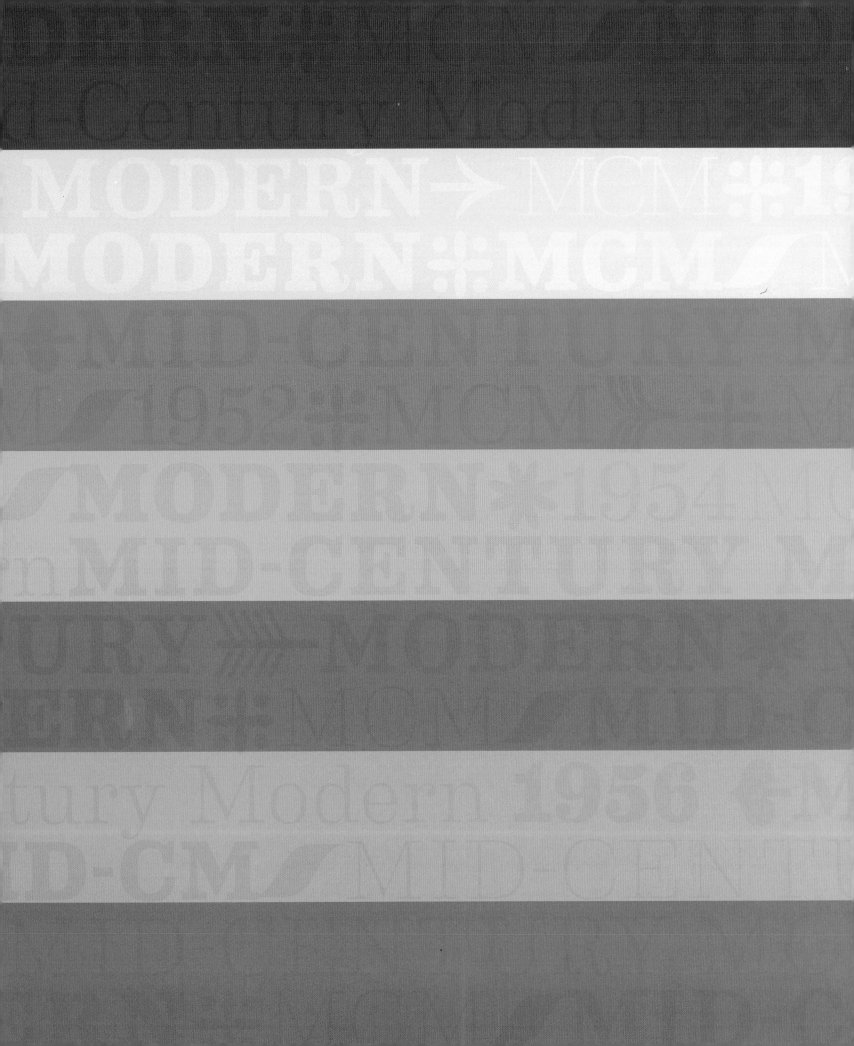